JAZZ AGE
CHICAGO

JAZZ AGE CHICAGO

CRUCIBLE OF MODERN AMERICA

JOSEPH GUSTAITIS

THE
History
PRESS

Published by The History Press
Charleston, SC
www.historypress.com

First published 2022

Manufactured in the United States

ISBN 9781467150798

Library of Congress Control Number: 2021949216

To John and Jeff, brothers, friends and fellow travelers on the journey through life.

CONTENTS

Introduction

MAKING AMERICA MODERN

The following objects are two everyday household items, used for the same thing—serving hot beverages—and they were made only about a generation apart. But they are from different worlds. The delicate Limoges porcelain tea set, circa 1900, was hand painted by "Miss Effie Dawes" of Chicago and was all about decoration, repose and exclusivity. The chrome and Bakelite coffee set from the early 1930s, designed by Michael McArdle of Chicago's Sunbeam Corporation, was all about streamlining, progress and middle-class aspiration. The two sets were part of a 2018–21 exhibition at the Chicago History Museum called "Modern by Design: Chicago Streamlines America," and their juxtaposition embodies the theme of the show: modernism. From approximately World War I to the first years of the Great Depression, Chicago's role in bringing modernism to American life was profound. These two sets, so seemingly commonplace, are symbolic of a cultural dynamism that was generated in Chicago and inspired historian Jonathan Mekinda to assert that the Windy City "made America modern."[1]

Consider another image—a postcard from the 1920s. It demonstrates how Chicago designers, in making America modern, applied the progressive style of the coffee set to much grander objects. The two skyscrapers portrayed on the postcard straddle Michigan Avenue, just south of the Chicago River. The building on the right, partially shown, is the ornate London Guarantee Building (1923). The plainer building on the left, 333 North Michigan Avenue, opened a mere five years later. Again, they were from two different

Above: Making America modern.
Photograph by the author.

Left: Postcard from the 1920s.
Author's collection.

worlds. The London Guarantee Building, with its Corinthian columns, is a backward-looking Beaux-Arts beauty. The much different 333 North Michigan is, like the coffee set, what we now call "Art Deco," although, in 1928, people didn't label it Art Deco, as that term was not widely used until the 1960s.[2] According to architecture historian Mike Hope, "The term Art Deco has become a catch-all nomenclature covering a period which most people would take to be between 1925 and 1939, but with many specialists now looking at the years 1910–1940."[3] In his international survey *Art Deco Architecture: The Interwar Period*, Hope, accounting for "national and regional variations," listed more than fifty terms observers used at the time to designate the innovative style; among them were *Zig-Zag Moderne*, *Ocean Liner Style*, *Streamline Beaux Arts*, *Classical Moderne*, *Stripped Neo-Classicism* and *Chicago School*. But most American contemporaries used the term *moderne*, a word with roots in 1920s Paris. In an effort to make the term American, others also used *jazz moderne* and *jazz modern*.

Books about Chicago in the early twentieth century tend to have titles such as *Murder City*; *Wicked City*; *Mayors, Madams, and Madmen*; *The Girls of Murder City*; *Gangland Chicago*; *Gangsters and Grifters*; *A Killing in Capone's Playground*; and *Al Capone's Beer Wars*.[4] This is certainly a valid approach. Crime and corruption were blatant in Chicago during the Jazz Age, and crime boss Al Capone was the most famous American in the world at the time. So, this book offers a vivid tour of the underworld, speakeasies, rumrunning and Prohibition. It examines the recurring question of whether Capone was a public benefactor or a public enemy, and it evaluates the forces that brought him down, including the famed Eliot Ness and his Untouchables. Nevertheless, to comprehend Chicago—and America—in the 1920s, what is required is a cultural history broader than crime-focused surveys. Although some of the events of Jazz Age Chicago have been sensationalized, they are better understood in their cultural context, when they were blamed on a creeping moral rot fueled by jazz. One cannot understand twentieth-century American culture without accounting for Chicago. To the *rat-tat-tat* of the gangster's machine gun (cleverly nicknamed "Chicago typewriter") and the squealing of a getaway car's tires, this book adds the blare of Louis Armstrong's cornet, the chug of a steam shovel digging the foundation of an Art Deco skyscraper and the roars of a Wrigley Field crowd.

If the first thesis of this book concerns Chicago's role in making America modern, the second, related proposition is that jazz, which was then modern music par excellence, reflected the nation's innovative outlook. In the 1920s, observers of American life considered jazz to be more than a type of music;

BIRTH OF "MODERNE" ART
When it was new, the style we now call "Art Deco" was termed "moderne," and the Russakov Company of Chicago fashionably stamped the word on the back of its classic Art Deco tray. *Author's collection.*

they saw it as a cultural attitude, a lens through which to observe and understand the transition they were experiencing. This book uses the idea of jazz as a lens, through which it will take snapshots of a city moving into the modern age. It focuses on phenomena that might seem unrelated but find common ground in jazz moderne.

When Jonathan Mekinda said Chicago "made America modern," he was thinking mostly of consumer goods. Chicago designers were instrumental in applying the Art Deco streamlined style to many household items—not only kitchen appliances but also furniture, watches, clocks, jewelry, bicycles, radios and so on. But this book argues that the 1920s was the first modern decade and that Chicago—as the locus of the Jazz Age outlook, an architectural laboratory, a center of modern design, a radio pioneer, an aviation leader, a musical capital, a home of bohemian culture, a sports hub and more—was a primary force in many of the developments that made it so. As the London Guarantee Building and 333 North Michigan show, in architecture, Chicagoans continued an already established tradition of architectural innovation with buildings that transitioned from the Beaux-Arts style to Art Deco. Today, as Mike Hope has put it, "Chicago possesses an absolute wealth of Art Deco buildings."[5] Meanwhile, Chicago builders developed a new form of housing for the working class: the bungalow, which represented the incorporation of modern technology into the home. Chicago radio pioneers invented the sitcom and the soap opera, two staples of American life, and it was in the Windy City—not New Orleans or New York—that jazz, the most American of musical styles, transitioned into an art form. Chicago also fostered a bohemian culture that was remarkably tolerant of gay rights and racial equality. The city produced a painter who arguably became the nation's greatest Black artist, and it played a decisive role in making professional sports one of the key elements of American culture (the term *jazz moderne* can be—and has been —applied to the Chicago sports scene). Finally, Chicago's Century of Progress Exposition of 1933–34 consolidated the triumph of the "streamlined" phase of Art Deco.

The population of Chicago almost doubled between 1900 and 1930, and the pace of new construction in the city was breathtaking. In 1923, the city effectively removed height restrictions on buildings—skyscrapers proliferated, and the supply of office space in the city nearly doubled.[6] With the opening of the Michigan Avenue Bridge in 1920, Chicago's mercantile district leaped over the river, leading to the construction of the "Magnificent Mile." Much of what visitors enjoy in Chicago today, like the Adler Planetarium, the Shedd Aquarium, Soldier Field, Buckingham Fountain and the building that houses the Field Museum, was created in the Jazz Age.

By the end of the Jazz Age, Chicago was not just a city of national and international importance, but it was in the first rank of the first modern decade. Chicago was a city of Prohibition and gangsters, but at its heart, it had a jazz spirit. And as the first chapter argues, this jazz spirit was the spirit of American culture and the driver of the first modern decade.

1

JAZZ AND THE SPIRIT OF THE TIMES

On December 23, 1921, the Chicago Symphony Orchestra premiered a new composition—*Krazy Kat: A Jazz Pantomime*. The reviewers loved it. One commented that the composer "has elevated jazz to a position in the great orchestra."[7] It was the first classical composition to use the word "jazz" in its title, and it came a little more than two years before George Gershwin's *Rhapsody in Blue*, usually considered the first concert work to adapt jazz to the classical idiom.[8]

The composer of *Krazy Kat* was a Chicagoan named John Alden Carpenter (1876–1951). Carpenter's first notable composition was the popular *Adventures in a Perambulator* (1915), a tonal depiction of a day in the life of a baby. Two years later, he presented his *Piano Concertino*, which has been called "a landmark in American concert music" for its incorporation of ragtime and Latin rhythms.[9] After *Krazy Kat* came another jazz-infused ballet, *Skyscrapers* (1926). The reviews of *Skyscrapers* were enthusiastic; one hailed its description of the "vital forces" of "our distinctive national life." Given that *Skyscrapers* celebrates the towers of Carpenter's hometown, he might be thought of as not only a jazz composer but also as the first (and probably only) Art Deco composer.

Looking Through the Lens of Jazz

Carpenter's era is sometimes known as the "Roaring Twenties," but it is probably better known as the "Jazz Age," a term coined by F. Scott

[9]

JAZZ AT THE CONCERT HALL
Chicago's own John Alden Carpenter, shown in a caricature by artist/writer Gene Markey, was the first composer to use jazz in classical music—not George Gershwin, as is commonly said. *Author's collection.*

Fitzgerald in 1922. The cultural history of Jazz Age Chicago includes such new forms of expression as radio, movies, pop music, sports and mass-circulation magazines and newspapers (*Krazy Kat* was based on a comic strip). By thinking of "jazz" as not only a type of music but also as a cultural sensibility, the term can apply to other phenomena. For example, the term *jazz moderne* became current as people, when confronted with Art Deco's zigzags, instinctively thought of jazz. The futurist architect Le

Corbusier, for example, remarked that skyscrapers represented "hot jazz in stone and steel." The Black painter Archibald Motley Jr. created genre scenes depicting Chicago's Bronzeville neighborhood, and when we see a Motley painting of a cabaret, we need to imagine jazz playing in the background. The art historian Richard J. Powell has called Motley "the quintessential jazz painter, without equal."[10]

A relationship between jazz and the American spirit is the subject of a collection of essays edited by Robert G. O'Meally titled *The Jazz Cadence of American Culture*; in the introduction, O'Meally, the author, says "that in this electric process of American artistic exchange—in the intricate, shape-shifting equation that is the twentieth-century American experience in culture—the factor of jazz music recurs over and over and over again: jazz dance, jazz poetry, jazz painting, jazz film, and more. Jazz as metaphor, jazz as model, jazz as relentlessly powerful cultural influence, jazz as cross-disciplinary beat or *cadence*."[11]

The energy of the Jazz Age was nervous, optimistic and even frivolous. F. Scott Fitzgerald wrote that the era began in the spring of 1920 in a mood of "general hysteria." Americans were riding a wave of innovation and saw no reason it should stop. For many, jazz meant change. As one analyst has written, "For many Americans, to argue about jazz was to argue about the nature of change itself."[12] Another aspect that reflected this energy was the speed of that change. As music historian Rob Kapilow has written, "We tend to think of the twenty-first century as a time when new technologies make older ones obsolete at dizzying speed, but the pace of invention in the 1920s and '30s makes contemporary innovation seem slow by comparison."[13] The songwriter Irving Berlin, who knew as much as anyone about the music of the time, said jazz reflected the "rhythmic beat of our everyday lives. Its swiftness is interpretive of our verve and speed and ceaseless activity."[14] The people of the era weren't ashamed of indulging in a little zaniness, and one indication of their playful energy was the enthusiasm with which they welcomed fads or crazes. Using the word *craze* to describe something of intense, short-lived popularity was a creation of the Jazz Age.[15] Among these fads were flagpole sitting, crossword puzzles, marathon dancing and Mah Jongg.

The enthusiasm for sports in the 1920s also reflected a jazz sensibility. Many of the sports stars brought something different, something more "energetic" than what had been customary. Babe Ruth is the most obvious example, but Lars Anderson, the biographer of football star Red Grange, spoke of Grange's "jazzlike improvisation on the field."[16] Historian Davarian

L. Baldwin argues that the style of today's basketball and football is derived from the jazz culture of Chicago's Black community on the South Side:

The jazz music accompaniment that drew fans to the unproven commodities of basketball and professional football directly influenced the style of play. The Black "shimmy" and the appropriately named "jukin" running style on the gridiron were powerfully influenced by the "rabbles" at half-times and musical rhythms during the games. Some assert that the transition of basketball from primarily a set-shot to a jump-shot game was heavily influenced by the after-party jazz music contexts of the Savoy Ballroom, with their "air-walking" lindy hop dancers. The jazz parlance "hot playing" was used as early as 1919 to describe the sped-up "racehorse" style of basketball performed by Virgil Blueitt and the Wabash (YMCA) Outlaws.[17]

The music critic Winthrop Sergeant contended that jazz was a key indication of the split from European culture that Americans achieved in the twentieth century, and he argued that the jazz spirit, with its "feverish activity," is quintessentially American. "It is not surprising," he wrote, "that a society that has evolved the skyscraper, the baseball game, and the 'happy ending' movie, should find its most characteristic musical expression in an art like jazz." He argued that Americans value a sense of incompleteness, because the typical American is an "incurable progressive." John A. Kouwenhoven, a prolific writer on American culture, argued that Chicago's urban skyline of skyscrapers gives the impression of unity in diversity—"Once steel cage construction has passed a certain height, the effect of transactive upward motion has been established; from there on, the point at which you cut it off is arbitrary and makes no difference." Incompleteness is central to the aesthetic. Americans, he says, favor things that are in development, that are "open-ended"—like an urban street grid in which thoroughfares have no fixed termination, a skyscraper or a performance by a jazz ensemble.[18]

Finally, in the 1920s, jazz, along with cigarettes, short skirts and bootleg alcohol, was considered a means of rebellion—against European standards of culture, against Victorian morality, against parental mores and "small-town" values. When critics—both Black and White—denigrated jazz as vulgarity practiced by incompetents, that only made the music more attractive to the flappers and their beaus. As the voice of a new generation, jazz brought a lot of cultural weight along with it and became the sound and spirit of the age that spanned the interwar years.[19]

THE FIRST MODERN DECADE

Today, we relate to the citizens of the Jazz Age because they were like us. The 1920s was an era in which Americans created and came to share a national pattern of preferences and leisure and when consumption came to characterize the American way of life. The 1920s was the "decade in which Americans firmly embraced a new manner of living."[20]

The British novelist L.P. Hartley famously wrote, "The past is a foreign country." But if we were to travel back in time to the Jazz Age, we wouldn't find it especially foreign. People in the 1920s had electric lights, flushable toilets, electric commuter trains and automobiles—in 1920 there were 9 million cars in the United States, and in 1930, there were 23 million cars and four out of every five families owned a car.[21] People rode on rapid transit systems, worked in offices in tall buildings with elevators and typed on keyboards. They had records and pop music, they danced in clubs, they went to restaurants and movie theaters and they were big sports fans. Radio was creating a national celebrity culture, and they loved sitcoms and soap operas. Advertising was unavoidable, largely due to radio, newspapers and magazines. Even air travel was becoming possible—Chicago's Midway Airport opened in 1926. Finally, a youth culture was emerging. Movies, sports, automobiles and jazz appealed to the young, and stories were already circulating about teenagers being addicted to telephones. The median age was only twenty-four, and two-thirds of the population was thirty-five or younger.[22]

The initiation of a mass consumer culture in the Jazz Age brought "standardizing and flattening processes" that "eroded regional distinctions."[23] Forces like movies, radio and mass-circulation magazines encouraged a sense of a common national identity. When an occurrence, such as a hero's welcoming parade or a boxing match, was broadcast live on the radio, the whole country shared it simultaneously. "For the first time in the nation's history, one could realistically talk of a national audience for a political, sports, or other event."[24]

Many of today's supermarket staples were introduced in the Jazz Age; among them were Wonder Bread, Peter Pan peanut butter, Welch's grape jelly, Butterfinger candy bars, Wheaties, Rice Krispies, Land O'Lakes butter, Oscar Meyer wieners, flavored yogurt, Velveeta cheese, La Choy foods, Popsicles, 7UP and Sanka.[25] Nonedible products included Scotch tape, Listerine, Band-Aids, Drano, Kleenex and Brillo.[26] And the list goes on and on—customers were buying these items in supermarkets. People were also consuming fast food—the White Castle hamburger chain opened in 1921, and Howard Johnson's followed four years later. Women no longer had to sew their own clothes—they bought them in stores or ordered them from catalogs. Because of the low prices, fashions were remarkably egalitarian. As the social theorist Stuart Chase explained at the time, "Only a connoisseur can distinguish Miss Astorbilt on Fifth Avenue from her father's stenographer or secretary."[27] It took only a year or two for designer fashions to travel from Paris to the Chicago-based Sears catalog: "For as little as $8.98, a young farm girl living miles outside Duluth, Minnesota, could purchase a silk flat crepe skirt and chemise of the latest flapper style; another 95 cents bought her a real 'Clara Bow' hat to match."[28] Women were also becoming keen users of cosmetics; in 1927, they spent nearly $2 billion on cosmetic products.[29] Lipstick became fashionable with the invention of the swivel-up tube in 1923. The popularity of makeup created a new profession and a new word—*beautician*.

Women began shaving their armpits, a practice made necessary by the revealing clothes and vigorous arm actions of the new dances. The downside of the fashion mania was a concern about weight. The flapper styles stressed slimness, and critics began lamenting the pressure being put on young women to shed pounds while tobacco companies promoted cigarettes as a way of staying thin. It was in the Jazz Age that Americans began their obsession with dieting.

As for modernism in the arts, by the Jazz Age, Chicagoans had grown familiar with cubism, abstract painting and Postimpressionism—they had seen these styles as early as 1913, when the New York Armory Show, which had introduced modern European art to the United States, traveled to Chicago's Art Institute. In 1912, Chicagoan Harriet Monroe founded *Poetry* magazine, which championed the works of such modernists as T.S. Eliot, Ezra Pound, Carl Sandburg and Wallace Stevens. In the 1920s, the Chicago Symphony Orchestra gave the American premieres of works by such modern composers as Gustav Mahler, Ottorino Respighi and Frederick Delius. As for popular music, today's pop music is certainly different from what it was in the 1920s, but contemporary pop stars can (and do) sing Cole Porter songs that don't sound particularly old-fashioned.

The clothing of the 1920s was, in many ways, surprisingly contemporary; many of the outfits wouldn't look strange today. Men still wear suits and ties, and women still wear short skirts and short hair. A man today could wear a Brooks Brothers striped tie from the 1920s and not get a second look; a woman could do the same with a Jazz Age blouse. In 1927, the French tennis player René Lacoste introduced a polo shirt with a crocodile

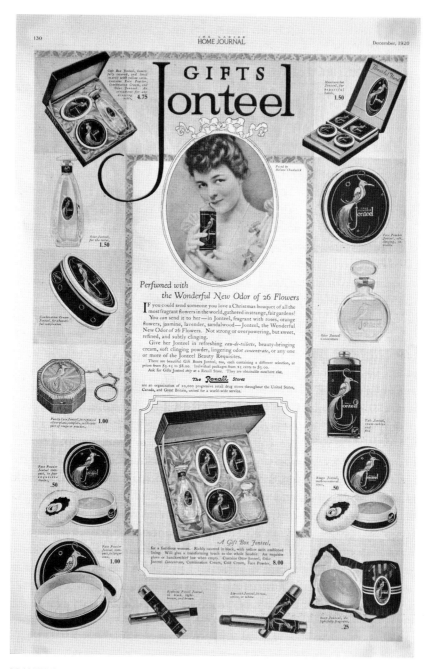

BEAUTY IN A BOTTLE

In the Jazz Age, American women began taking to cosmetics is a big way. By 1927, Americans were spending more on beauty products than they were on electricity. *Author's collection.*

SMOKE AND STAY YOUNG
Jazz Age women embraced
modern liberation by taking up
cigarettes, and shrewd tobacco
companies cleverly promoted
their products as a way of
staying slim. *Author's collection.*

on it; men still buy them. In October 2016, the *New York Times* reported
that hairdressers in Europe were striving to create a hairstyle like the one
worn by Josephine Baker, the Black American performer who was the toast
of Jazz Age Paris. The fact that this was a ninety-year-old hairstyle did not
even provoke comment.

Commentators on contemporary America who discuss the effects of
the sexual revolution of the 1960s typically fail to mention that this was
the nation's second sexual revolution. The first began around World War
I and was in full swing during the Jazz Age. Liberated women raised their
hemlines (a lot), wore "peekaboo" blouses, smoked cigarettes in public,
necked in automobiles and bobbed their hair (women even started going to
barbershops). The terms for these "new women" included *vamp*, *gold digger*
and *jazz baby*. Before the Jazz Age, women rarely went to bars, but during
Prohibition, women patronized and were welcome in speakeasies. "Dating"
became the most common way for young couples to get together. Previously,
young men were expected to "call on" young ladies at their homes, where

a watchful parent hovered nearby. By the 1920s, young couples were going out, with the automobile serving as both means of transportation and a space for intimacy. This evolution occurred because the Jazz Age generation was the first in America to grow up with the internal combustion engine as an everyday thing. By the mid-1920s, the nation's factories were producing nearly 3 million automobiles every year (Ford alone made 1.7 million—the price of a Model T had dropped to less than $300).[30] By 1929, America's annual automobile production had reached 5.3 million.[31] Between 1920 and 1930, the number of automobile registrations in Chicago soared from 90,000 to nearly 500,000, and it was already becoming next to impossible to get a parking spot in the downtown area of any major U.S. city.[32] Traffic jams were becoming an inescapable nuisance not only in Chicago but also in New York, Detroit and Los Angeles. Many Chicago streets were widened to accommodate cars, including twenty-nine miles of Western Avenue and twenty miles of Ashland Avenue.[33]

CRUNCH TIME
By the 1920s, traffic jams were becoming a major problem in Chicago, as shown in this scene on LaSalle Street. The *Chicago Tribune* reported that congestion in the Loop was costing the city $100,000 a day. *Courtesy of the Museum of Innovation and Science.*

If we were to be magically transported to 1927, things would seem different, but they wouldn't seem alien. It would be different if we found ourselves in, say, 1870, when light came from candles, people commuted on horseback, toilets were located in backyards and women wore bustles and whalebone corsets. Economist and historian Robert J. Gordon has argued that five "great inventions" transformed the world in the decades after 1870 in a way unparalleled in history: the internal combustion engine, electricity, chemicals and pharmaceuticals, urban sanitation and modern communication.[34] To live before those developments was to live in the pre-modern world. To live after them, especially after they became available to the middle class in the 1920s, was to live in the modern age.

Although the people of the Jazz Age were modern, they were, of course, not like us in all respects. Most viewed homosexuality as a sin, a crime or a mental illness (or all three), and few considered it wrong that baseball was segregated. Surprisingly—given Chicago's large population of Catholics, Black people, immigrants and Jews—the racist, anti-Catholic, anti-foreigner, antisemitic Ku Klux Klan was successful in the Windy City in the early 1920s. Chicago had the largest Klan membership (eighty thousand) of any American metropolis at the time, and crosses were burned within the city's limits. The Klan's prominence in Chicago, however, was brief. The city government condemned the group, and a Catholic newspaper published the names, addresses and occupations of a large number of Chicago Klan members. By 1925, the group had nearly disappeared from the city. And, as we will see, liberal attitudes toward same-sex attraction and race relations were forming.

In the following chapters, you will meet people who solved crossword puzzles, went to the movies, played pinball, danced and loved sports. They are our ancestors, but they are also our neighbors.

INTERLUDE: THE FLAPPER CAPITAL

In the Jazz Age, every American city had flappers. But only Chicago had *Flapper* magazine, which arguably made the city the capital of flappermania.

The flapper—that sexually liberated, bobbed-haired female rebel—appeared before World War I, but she became one of

The Flapper, August 1922.
Author's collection.

the most enduring symbols of the Roaring Twenties. She was the pivot of America's first sexual revolution.

The *Flapper's* offices were located in the Ogden Building at 192 North Clark Street. The masthead of the magazine read "Not for Old Fogies." The managing editor was Thomas Levish, but most of the sassy content seems to have come from Associate Editor Myrna Serviss, a flapper herself. An example of this is "The Psychology of Knees": "For the first time since civilization began, the world is learning that girls, women, females, maidens, and damsels have KNEES. Nevertheless, it's the naked truth. And it's becoming more evident every day. 'Tain't necessary to roll the sox to disclose them. The short dresses have revealed them to a gasping world. And oh, what a shock!" Serviss created the "National Flappers Flock" and urged readers to write in to learn how to form a local chapter. *Flapper* had an advice column, celebrity gossip, jokes (or "Flapperisms") and fashion advice. It also organized a flapper beauty contest.

The magazine had a brief life—a mere seven months in 1922—as short-lived as any fad of the era.

2

A VISIT TO JAZZ AGE CHICAGO

(Chi-CA-go)
It's a crescent-shaped town, 26 miles by 15, along a great lake that's begun to
weaken and recede. No wonder.
An unchallenged murder record—a splendid university—hobo capital to the
country—railroad ruler, corn baron, liquor king—and the finest of grand opera.
Altogether the most zestful spectacle on this sphere.
—Chicagoan, *August 27, 1927*

Imagine you're a traveler in the late 1920s pulling into LaSalle Street
Station on the New York Central's Twentieth Century Limited. A shiny
Model T taxi quickly takes you to your downtown hotel—the Palmer
House maybe, or the Congress, or perhaps the Stevens, the largest hotel
in the world. If you're like the British reporter W.L. George, who visited
Chicago in 1923, the first thing that might strike you is the racket. Chicago
is a busy place.

> *My first impression of Chicago was indeed noise.…I had still to realize*
> *the impact upon the human ear of two lines of trolley cars running over*
> *cobbles, on wheels that are never oiled; this, combined with several hundreds*
> *of motor vehicles with their throttles open; this combined with a double line*
> *of elevated railways whose couplings are never oiled; and this combined*
> *with a policeman who acts as master of the revels by means of a whistle!*
> *What a whistle! A steam whistle? A steam policeman? In Chicago, you*
> *can never tell.*[35]

SEEING THE SIGHTS

What did visitors want to see? In 1929, Chicago reporter John Drury wrote that the highlights of his city included "the Field Museum, Navy Pier, the University of Chicago, Wacker Drive, the great connected park and boulevard system, Upper Michigan Avenue, the new Buckingham Memorial Fountain, McKinlock campus of Northwestern University, Soldiers' Field stadium, the Art Institute, and the new Civic Opera building and plaza." Remarkably, all these sights still exist.[36] A visitor to the Art Institute, named Arthur Everett Shipley, was amazed to discover "a whole room filled with Monets!" (Chicagoans, most notably the wealthy Bertha Palmer, were early adopters of French Impressionism.) The *Rand McNally Chicago Guide to Places of Interest in the City and Environs* (1927) ticks off the major things to see, beginning with, "The business section of Chicago is the first point of interest, for it is the feature that is most strikingly metropolitan." A section titled "Some of the Notable Buildings" lists, first, the Wrigley Building, followed by the Medinah Temple, the Auditorium Building, the Rand McNally Building, the Rookery, Orchestra Hall, the Straus Building, the Chicago Temple Building, the London Guarantee Building and the Illinois Merchant Bank Building. Some of the sights are familiar today (Grant Park, Soldier Field, Lincoln Park, Lake Shore Drive, Newberry Library and Hull-House), while others are gone (the Fish Hatchery, the Caravel, the Coliseum, the Masonic Temple Building, the John Crerar Library Building and the Japanese Buildings in Lincoln Park).

In 1921, the *Chicago Tribune* called State Street "the largest shopping district on earth." Its list of stores begins with the greatest, Marshall Field & Co., and continues, heading south, with Charles A. Stevens & Bros.; Mandel Brothers; Carson, Pirie, and Scott; Hillman's; the Boston Store; the Fair; and Rothschild's. The story says the intersection of Madison and State Streets has "the densest pedestrian traffic in the world"; others called it simply "the busiest corner in the world." When visitors get to Randolph Street, they've reached Chicago's "Rialto," where one can see "no less than seven theaters—the Apollo, the Colonial, the Woods, the Garrick, the Olympic, Powers, and the Cort."

Imagine you're in 1921 Chicago. If you cross the Chicago River on the new bridge, you'll find yourself on upper Michigan Avenue, which was then undergoing frantic construction. Start at the terracotta Wrigley Building, gaze at the Tribune Tower and then proceed through an exclusive shopping district, passing by the Allerton House and the striking new Palmolive

RAND McNALLY CHICAGO GUIDE

TO PLACES OF INTEREST IN THE CITY AND ENVIRONS

FIFTY CENTS

SO MUCH TO SEE
Tourists in 1920s Chicago had several guidebooks to choose from, including the *Rand McNally Chicago Guide* (1927), which called Chicago "the meeting place of the world." *Author's collection.*

Building, and end at the Drake Hotel. Proceed a bit farther north along the lakefront, and you're in the Gold Coast. It's a neighborhood where no respectable visitor brings an umbrella to another's home (it shows the visitor had walked, which isn't done). In the Gold Coast, you find "the imposing stone mansions, with their green lawns and wrought-iron-grilled doorways, of Chicago's wealthy aristocracy and industrial and financial kings."[37] Just south of the Gold Coast in Streeterville are massive, posh apartment houses, where flats can be rented out for a staggering $1,000 a month ($15,000 in today's money). No one knows their neighbors.[38]

Venture west of State Street and Michigan Avenue and you're in the free-spirited neighborhood known as "Tower Town" (named after the nearby Water Tower). This is the turf of Chicago's artistic community—bookstores, art galleries and cafés animated with talk of the current "isms" (Marxism, cubism, futurism, Freudianism and so on) abound. Keep going west, and you find the "furnished room" district. Most of the roomers have clerical jobs, like accounting and secretarial work, and they walk to their jobs in the Loop. There is also a population of students there. Continue heading

"CHICAGO'S RIALTO"
Downtown Randolph Street offered seven major theaters, plentiful restaurants and, for
those in the know, more than a few speakeasies. *Author's collection.*

VANISHING STREETSCAPE
"Imposing stone mansions" still stood in Chicago's Gold Coast in the 1920s, but encroaching apartment buildings would soon replace nearly all of them. *Author's collection.*

toward the north branch of the Chicago River, and you'll reach the "slum." This area of dilapidated houses and tenements, dubbed "Little Hell," has been successively inhabited by the Irish, the Germans, the Swedish and now the Sicilians, although some Black individuals have started to move in, along with a few Chinese people.

If you are interested in Chicago's "melting pot," you might explore the Near West Side. West of Union Park is the "Fulton Colored District." Also in the West Side is the Greek enclave around Halsted and Harrison Streets and the large expanse of "Little Italy" centered on West Taylor Street. The Jewish District is in the area of Halsted Street and Roosevelt Road. There, you'll find Glickman's Palace Theater and Barron & Son's restaurant, a hangout for Jewish writers and intellectuals. A little farther south is what is called the "Ghetto"—the Jewish commercial district on Maxwell Street, where there are "over two thousand vendors selling from stores, stalls, pushcarts, wagons, and boxes."[39] Street musicians play here, and you might catch someone playing that lively new music called the blues. When you get down around Eighteenth Street, you are in "Pilsen"—the habitat of Czech immigrants. The main Black area of the city is Bronzeville, which stretches from just south of the Loop, centered on State Street, to about Fifty-Fifth Street. Although much of the housing is crowded and substandard, a sizeable Black middle-class population lives in fine, solid homes. The core

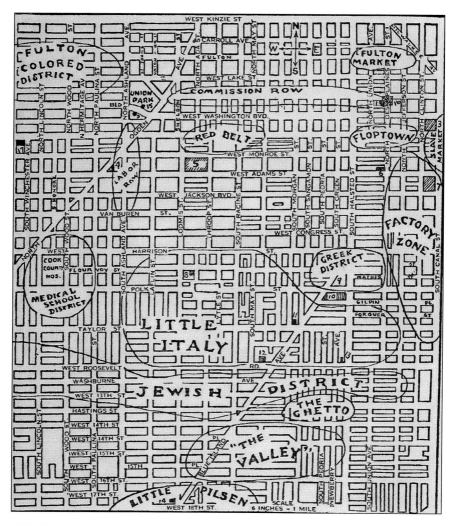

METROPOLITAN MOSAIC
Chicago's leftist leanings and melting pot of ethnic groups could be seen at their most colorful on the West Side, as shown in this map from 1928. The "Slave Market" was where unemployed laborers could find work in distant parts of the country and then take public transportation to a nearby terminal. *Author's collection.*

of the district is the "Stroll"—a brightly lit stretch of State Street that has dozens of nightclubs, cabarets, cafés and restaurants. When you go west of Bronzeville and enter Bridgeport, you're in the enclave of the Irish, who figure so prominently in Chicago politics.

The Swedes mostly congregate in the North Side neighborhoods of Lake View and Andersonville. The heart of the Polish community (or

"Polonia") is the intersection of Division Street, Milwaukee Avenue, and Ashland Avenue. The Germans have been keeping a low profile since they came into disfavor during World War I, but their community is still large and there is plenty of lager and wurst to be found along Lincoln and North Avenues on the North Side. The Mexican community in Chicago is small but growing, especially since Mexican workers were brought in as strikebreakers during the great steel strike of 1919. There are now three main places of Mexican settlement—on the West Side, in the "Back of the Yards" area near the packinghouses and in South Chicago and Irondale, where the steel mills are located.

AN EXPANDING METROPOLIS

In the nineteenth century, Chicago was the fastest-growing city in the world (probably in history), and in the 1920s, its growth continued. The population nearly doubled between 1900 and 1930 (from 1.7 million to 3.4 million), and by 1930, "the entire city area, except for some small patches mainly on its fringes, had been occupied."[40] Between 1918 and 1928, there was more construction in Chicago than in all the previous years of its history, and land values in the Loop doubled.[41] Construction costs were dropping, and real estate profits were climbing. Developers devised ways of financing construction through real estate bond issues, which meant they could put up new buildings without having to use their own money.[42] The Chicago Zoning Commission reported that more than twice as many residents lived in apartments than in houses, and many more building permits were given for apartment buildings than for single-family houses.[43] Yet single-family homes also proliferated, and large areas of the city became known as a "bungalow belt." Chicago's lakefront was being rescued from developers, expanded, and made home to new public institutions. Eight miles of parks and beaches were established south of Grant Park, and on the North Side, Oak Street Beach was created and Lincoln Park was expanded by a landfill. The construction of the Field Museum (1919), Shedd Aquarium (1930) and Adler Planetarium (1930) gave Chicago an unparalleled museum campus.[44] One of the city's most heralded developments was the opening of Wacker Drive, a double-decked ornamental street that ran along the south bank of the Chicago River from Michigan Avenue to Lake Street, on October 20, 1926. The new thoroughfare soon became the site of some of Chicago's finest skyscrapers.

AMERICA'S CITY OF LIGHT
In the 1920s, Chicago aspired to be "the best-lighted city in the world." A Chicago company, Curtis Lighting, specialized in indirect illumination and floodlighting, which helped turn city buildings into nocturnal showpieces. *Courtesy of the Library of Congress.*

The city's VIPs were determined to make Chicago "the best-lighted city in the world." In October 1926, 140 new extra-bright streetlights were illuminated on State Street.[45] Beginning with the Wrigley Building (1924), it became stylish to illuminate all or part of new buildings. The Curtis Lighting Company, founded by Chicagoan Augustus Curtis, was the "pioneer of indirect illumination" in the United States. Other major sources of street illumination were the many new movie palaces. Especially remarkable was Buckingham Fountain (1927), which was lit with a fantastic spectacle of changing patterns of colored lights produced by the "Lumitone" system.

SPORTS AND STOCKYARDS

Chicago had two major league baseball teams: the Cubs at Wrigley Field and the White Sox at Comiskey Park. The Sox were having a rough decade—they hadn't finished higher than fifth place since 1920. The Cubs also struggled throughout most of the 1920s, but they went on to the World Series in 1929 and 1932. The best team in town might have been Rube Foster's American Giants, an all-Black baseball team founded in 1911. The team won the championship of the Negro National League in 1920, 1921, 1922, 1926, 1927, 1932 and 1933. The major college football teams played at the University of Chicago and Northwestern University. The Chicago Bears football team was just getting started, but then they signed Red Grange, the greatest college player of the era. In 1926, Chicago businessman Frederic McLaughlin founded a professional hockey team and gave it the nickname of his old World War I army division—the Black Hawks.

Perhaps the most popular tourist attraction was the Union Stock Yard. Many tourists recorded their impressions, and many were appalled, amazed and awestruck. W.L. George, who gave such an eloquent description of Chicago's noise, also left a vivid account of a meatpacking plant:

> *To watch an animal go from the pen to the tin is an extraordinary experience. You see it killed; it falls; a conveyor carries it away. It is flayed while you wait. It disappears. Then, suddenly, it is an open carcass; it passes the veterinary; in a few seconds, it is cut up, and hurriedly, you follow the dwindling carcass that is no longer an ox but fragments of meat; you see the meat shredded; in another room, the manicured girls are filling the shreds into tins, and the tin is closed and labeled. The thing that astounds is the quiet officialdom of this murder. It is as if nothing had happened. Death is so swift, the evidence of tragedy so soon gone, that one feels no shock…life becomes merely a raw material. That is Chicago.[46]*

The stockyards are a reminder that Chicago is a workingman's town. In 1920, 40 percent of those gainfully employed were "engaged in manufacturing and mechanical industries."[47] The largest industries in Chicago were meatpacking and steel. International Harvester had a half dozen facilities in the city, turning out agricultural equipment, and the Pullman Company, a manufacturer of railroad cars (especially sleeping cars) was at its peak. One-third of the radios in the United States were being made in Chicago; other humming Chicago industries were printing and the making of clothing and furniture.

RESTAURANTS OF EVERY KIND

Because Chicagoans today can sample cuisines from all around the world, they might assume that their great-grandparents had fewer options. But Chicago in the 1920s offered a great many more dining choices than one might think.

The current restaurant culture has its roots in the 1920s—the number of restaurants in the United States tripled between 1919 and 1929. Some high-end restaurants might have suffered because they could no longer legally serve liquor, but popular quick-service restaurants, like diners, cafeterias, lunchrooms, hamburger joints and automats, thrived.[48] And despite Prohibition, Chicago still had fine-dining establishments with French décor and imported linens. Department store restaurants had surprisingly good food, and the city's grand railroad stations also offered many places to grab a bite.

Chain restaurants were then transforming dining. During the 1920s, Thompson's, which was started in Chicago in 1891, was a national restaurant chain with forty-nine restaurants in the Windy City alone.[49] Then there were the Triangle Restaurants (later Toffenetti's); the Loop contained six. According to reporter John Drury, "Foreign visitors to Chicago claim that the Triangle Restaurants are the most typical dining places of the United States....And I agree with them."[50] "Toothpick Row" along Clark Street offered a great many cafeterias, a food service that seems to have been invented in Chicago, and the country's first "themed" restaurant was probably the Rainbo Seafood Grotto on Dearborn Street, a nautical extravaganza that flaunted a real ship's rail, life preservers and plentiful portholes.

Steakhouses, for which Chicago is now famous, began to catch on with the opening of the Stock Yard Inn, a vast hotel/restaurant complex on South Halsted Street, near the stockyards, in 1913. In its Sirloin Room, diners could brand their initials into the steak of their choice before sending it to the kitchen to be cooked. Other places to eat steaks included Harding's Colonial Room on South Wabash, the Brevoort and Little Jack's (both on West Madison), Kau's on South Wells and Bollard & Frazier's Chop House on West Lake Street. The top-of-the-line steakhouse, however, was most likely Pete's Steaks on North Dearborn, although some swore by the steaks at Goldstein's on West Fourteenth Street, where they were broiled Jewish Romanian–style over a charcoal grill and accompanied by salad, pickles and caraway rye bread.

A few free spirits in Tower Town opened cozy cafés, restaurants and tea shops. A reviewer for the *Chicago Tribune* noted that these dining places were developing a newer, lighter American cuisine but disapproved of their tendency to excessively decorate the food—"ornamental combinations of mayonnaise and fruits, fluffy desserts topped by the ubiquitous and ruby-hued Maraschino cherry."[51] At the Noose Coffee Shop on Hubbard Street, the owner plastered the walls with pictures of criminals and donated the "last meal" to felons who were hanged in the nearby county jail.

Chicago's ethnic restaurants included Filipino (Manila Village Café), Middle Eastern (Arabian Café) and Hungarian (Ravenna) cuisines. The

PICK YOUR STEAK
At the Stock Yard Inn on South Halsted Street, near the stockyards, diners could brand their initials into the steak of their choice before sending it off to the kitchen. *Author's collection.*

Panhellenic Restaurant in Greektown boasted the city's finest lamb chops, while Spanish cuisine was available at the Casa de Alex. Mexican food could be found at El Puerto de la Vera Cruz, where Juan Malpica dished out his famous sopa de arroz, among other treats. Other ethnic eateries included the Holland Tea Room, the Idrott Swedish Co-operative Café and Glaser's, which was Czech. Lenard's, a Polish place on Milwaukee Avenue, was known for its zrazki po nelsonsku, a beef cutlet smothered in sour cream and mushrooms. La Louisiane, which offered New Orleans Creole cuisine, was noted for its pompano papillotte. German restaurants abounded—the Red Star Inn, the Berghoff and the Old Heidelberg Inn were the most famous. Meanwhile, a contemporary writer observed that Italian restaurants were "as thick on the near north side as cats in Siam."[52] Probably the most celebrated was Madame Galli's at 18 East Illinois Street. Another popular Italian eatery was Colosimo's, opened by the mobster "Big Jim" Colosimo in 1914. Chinese food could be found in Chinatown along Wentworth Street, where the restaurant Won Kow opened in 1928 (it lasted for ninety years). Outside of Chinatown, on the West Side, stood the enormous Golden Pumpkin, a Chinese restaurant that could seat one thousand patrons.[53]

Although these ethnic eateries had their devotees, most tourists would have dined downtown. One of the most heralded downtown eateries was Schlogl's, which was near the Chicago Daily News Building, and like the Algonquin Hotel in Manhattan, it had its "round table," where famous writers, like Carl Sandburg, Sherwood Anderson, Edgar Lee Masters, Ben Hecht, John Gunther, Robert Herrick and a slew of newspaper reporters, sat. Most visitors, however, would have wanted to patronize one of the top-of-the-line dining palaces, and two of the best in Jazz Age Chicago were the Tip Top Inn and Henrici's. The Tip Top Inn got its name from its lofty perch atop the Pullman Building on Michigan Avenue. Its proprietor, Adolf Hieronymus, a native of Frankfurt, Germany, opened it in 1893. The restaurant was divided into sections, such as the Colonial Room, Whist Room, Nursery, Italian Room, Flemish Room, Garden and the Charles Dickens Corner, each with suitable décor (the walls of the Whist Room, for example, sported jumbo playing cards). Herr Hieronymus offered a menu with no fewer than 109 specialties. Although the Tip Top Inn was one of the most famous restaurants in Jazz Age Chicago, its proprietor cited the Jazz Age as one of the factors in the demise of the business in 1931. As if Prohibition and the Depression weren't bad enough for business, younger diners had come

A ROOM FOR EVERY TASTE
The Tip Top Inn atop the Pullman Building was divided into different dining areas, each appropriately decorated. There was the Colonial Room, the Whist Room, the Nursery, the Italian Room, the Flemish Room, the Garden and, seen here, the Charles Dickens Corner. *Author's collection.*

to view the place as old-fashioned. The musicians at the Tip Top Inn still played Strauss waltzes, but the newer supper clubs offered jazz. Dancing had become more important than dining—which meant, Hieronymus said, "the passing of the gourmet."[54] Henrici's began as a downtown lunchroom as early as 1868, and in 1893, its German-born owner, Philip Henrici, opened a restaurant on Randolph Street in the theater district. He bucked the trend of featuring music—his famous motto was: "No orchestral din." The most popular main courses were hearty fare—beef à la mode, boiled brisket with horseradish sauce, braised short ribs, corned beef and cabbage—and the pastries were famous. Henrici's didn't close because of waning popularity, but it was razed in 1962 to make room for the massive Daley Center.

But one thing was not available in these restaurants and clubs: alcohol. For that, visitors would have to look elsewhere. That was not too difficult, as we shall see in the next chapter.

3

BEER FLATS AND BATHTUB GIN

DODGING PROHIBITION

The Eighteenth Amendment to the U.S. Constitution, which banned the manufacture, transportation and sale of alcoholic beverages, went into effect on January 17, 1920, and a new era began—one of bootlegging booze, speakeasies, organized crime and an unprecedented flouting of the law by formerly upstanding citizens.

Chances are that visitors to Chicago would have quickly discovered a downtown speakeasy. A "speakeasy" is simply an unlicensed bar or other place that sells illegal liquor. The idea was that you would whisper, or "speak easy," a password through a small window in the entrance door; it was advisable to keep the noise level low so as not to attract the attention of the law.

How many speakeasies operated in Chicago in the Jazz Age? It's impossible to say—anyone with a back room, some tables and chairs and a supply of booze could open one. The *Chicago Daily News* estimated there were 6,000, the *Chicago Tribune* said 10,000, but a survey conducted at the time by a Chicago crime-busting group reported 20,000—120 in Chicago's downtown Loop area alone.[55] Whatever the number, there were more speakeasies in Chicago in the 1920s than there are bars today.

Speakeasies were supposed to be secretive, but some were wide-open secrets. Even so, they tended to have rear or cellar entrances that were not immediately obvious, and their windows were often boarded up. Live music was sometimes offered, but some kind of soundproofing was usually attempted. Legitimate businesses in the front areas of the speakeasies sometimes served as covers. Gioco's in the South Loop, for example, was located in the back of a cold storage building, which not only concealed operations but also served as a place to keep the beer cold. The Twin Anchors Bar on the North Side was hidden behind a school supplies shop.

Of course, it wasn't necessary to open a speakeasy to sell alcohol. The *Tribune* reported in 1923 that Chicagoans were "buying their booze with their shoeshines, with their halibut steaks at the fishmongers, and even at the cobbler's."[56] Four years later, the *Chicagoan* magazine wrote, "Groceries, restaurants, cigar stores, laundries, barbershops, all are tempted to dabble a bit; a distressing number of such places do."[57] Many American cities sported "beer flats," apartments that had been converted into makeshift speakeasies. They were especially popular in Chicago, which, according to the show business newspaper *Variety*, contained sixteen thousand of them.[58]

Alcohol smuggling was a huge business. Adding together the Mexican border and the Great Lakes and the Atlantic and Pacific coasts, "the total distance vulnerable to smuggling was approximately 18,700 miles," according to historian Robert G. Folsom.[59] The proximity of Canada made it a prime source of smuggled alcohol, and the Great Lakes and the St. Lawrence River became the "highways of illegal bootleg commerce."[60] Most of the traffic was controlled by organized crime. Every day, as many as two thousand cases of alcohol traveled from Detroit—which brought in the liquor from Canada—to Chicago by boat, train or truck.[61] Corby's Whiskey, based in Ontario, produced five hundred gallons of alcohol a month in 1921; two years later it was producing fifty thousand.[62] A case of whiskey purchased in Quebec for $15 could sell for $120 in the United States.[63] The value of the beer and liquor brought through what was called the "Windsor-Detroit Funnel" was estimated to be some $40 million a year.[64] When the U.S. government stepped up its patrols on the Great Lakes and the St. Lawrence River, the result was more smuggling on "Rum Row," a fleet of ships moored along the Atlantic seaboard. Some smuggling vessels were close enough to the shore for day-trippers to sail out and pick up a case or two.[65] Traffic between Canada and Chicago went two ways: as booze came in, Americans went out in search of a drink, a practice known as "alcohol tourism." In the mid-1920s, some 2 million American cars crossed into Canada every year. One source estimates that by 1929, alcohol tourists were annually spending $300 million in Canada.[66] In many Canadian cities, especially Montreal, nightclubs catered to American tourists, and American performers and jazz musicians went north to find employment in these venues.

ALCOHOL TOURISM
The proximity of Canada to the United States made it a prime vacation destination during Prohibition, and humorous postcards were sold to visitors. By 1929, alcohol tourists were spending an estimated $300 million a year in Canada. *Author's collection.*

Much of the alcohol consumed in Chicago, however, was manufactured in the city—not smuggled. The average speakeasy owner typically got liquor from "connections"—in other words, gangsters. For example, racketeers organized a network of Sicilian families in Little Italy; each operated a mini still in their apartment. They earned a whopping $15 a day ($225 in today's money), and the entire neighborhood smelled of alcohol. Thousands of other Chicagoans also made liquor at home. Hardware stores sold portable stills for six dollars, and many Chicagoans have stories of family members who made wine in their basements. "Bathtub gin" got its name not because the liquor was made in the tub but because the bottles used were jugs or carboys—too tall to fit in the sink, necessitating the use of the bathtub faucet to top them up with water. And Al Capone, of course, made a fortune operating covert breweries, which, because they were so large, were way beyond the ability of ordinary folks to operate.

Law enforcement mostly looked the other way—Chicago was a "wide-open town." One historian of Prohibition wrote:

> *It can be argued that some of America's biggest villains during the Prohibition era were not the Al Capones, Johnny Torrios, Gus Morans,*

LAND OF OPPORTUNITY
"I'll be leaving in the summer, and I won't come back 'till fall / Goodbye Broadway, Hello Montreal"—so begins a tune from 1928 by the great songwriter Harry Warren. In several Canadian cities, nightclubs catered to American tourists and hired American musicians. *Author's collection.*

Dutch Schultzes, or Frank Costellos but the political bosses in New York, Chicago, and elsewhere who used the underworld to their considerable advantage, and the many venal, conniving police and law enforcement officials who supplemented their incomes with mobster money.[67]

Many police officers were on the mobsters' payrolls, and it was reported that 60 percent of Chicago's police force took part in the liquor business.[68] Even federal Prohibition commissioners were on the take and routinely warned speakeasy owners about upcoming raids.

Famous Chicago speakeasies included the Green Mill, the Planet Mars, the Club Royale, the Midnight Frolic, the Rendezvous, the Moulin Rouge and Colosimo's, founded by top mobster "Big Jim" Colosimo, Capone's predecessor. In 1920s Chicago, a bellhop might have directed you to 122 North Clark Street. We know about this place because it was raided, and a description was given in the *Chicago Tribune*. The building contained not one but two speakeasies—on the fourth and fifth floors. On the lower level, prohibition agents discovered "about thirty well-clad people drinking and laughing in the Capricorn Social Club. A polished bar was crowded and W.J. McElligott, the barkeep, was serving beer on tap, ale, wine, whisky, and gin." The lawmen then "dashed up one more flight and entered another noisy room, a speakeasy purported to be owned by Dan Monahan, a Loop figure for years, according to the agents." None of the customers were arrested, and only four proprietors were hauled off.[69]

Many speakeasy patrons were women. Before the 1920s, respectable women rarely went to bars. According to historian Mary Murphy, "Drinking in the late nineteenth and early twentieth centuries was one of the most gender-segregated activities in the United States." In the Jazz Age, nightlife became "heterosocial," as speakeasies welcomed female patrons. As Murphy put it, "Prohibition allowed women to rewrite the script of acceptable public behavior."[70] It also seems speakeasies were casual about underage drinking. In 1928, the president of the Chicago Board of Education bemoaned the "prevalence of speakeasies catering to public school children." Cited in the newspaper was one John Boozer, the felicitously named owner of a South Side candy store "less than 100 feet from the Coleman Elementary School" that sheltered "four jugs of moonshine."[71]

Most speakeasies were not cheap. One of the myths about Prohibition is that the country was awash in booze. The best evidence indicates that alcohol consumption declined by as much as 70 percent in the first years of Prohibition, although it then crept back up until the early 1930s, when it

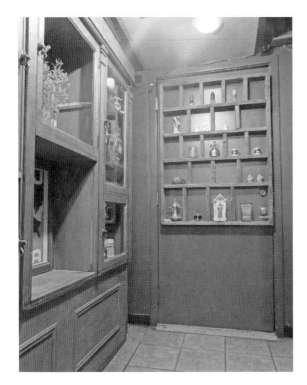

SHHH!
It's doubtful many people were fooled, but during Prohibition, the venerable Green Door Tavern on Orleans Street in Chicago actually hid its barroom behind a green door. *Photograph by the author.*

was about 60 to 70 percent of what it had been before 1920.[72] One historian has written that "Prohibition should actually be considered to have been a relatively successful experiment."[73] Lauterback's, a Capone-owned speakeasy in Cicero, might serve as example of prices in an average joint—whiskey was $0.75 a shot, beer $0.35 a stein and wine $0.30 a glass (one exception: policemen drank for free).[74] Whiskey at $0.75 might sound reasonable, but in 1925, the average hourly wage for a skilled workman (carpenter, painter) was about $1.30. The average person, then, usually relied on home brews, and some of it caused paralysis, blindness or even death. A glass of what was called "smoke," which was often poisonous, went for $0.10.[75] In that sense, the success of Prohibition depended on class. The English writer G.K. Chesterton, who visited the United States in the early 1920s, viewed Prohibition as a way of subjugating the lower orders of society. America, he wrote, is "where the wealthy are all at this moment sipping their cocktails and discussing how much harder labourers can be made to work if only they can be kept from festivity."[76]

At the apex of the illegal alcohol trade in Chicago was the legendary mob boss Al Capone, to whom we now turn.

INTERLUDE: A CHICAGOAN IN PARIS

Her real name was Ada Smith, but everyone called her "Bricktop." She was a Black woman with a Scotch-Irish grandmother, who accounted for her brassy russet-red hair. She got her start in Chicago but won her fame in Paris, where, for the bon vivants and night owls, she was the messenger who carried the Jazz Age from Chicago to France.

Bricktop was born in Alderson, West Virginia, in 1894. When her father died, her mother relocated to Chicago. Bricktop began performing in her mid-teens, first in Black-owned theaters and then in saloons. By 1922, she was singing in Harlem, and two years later, Bricktop was invited to perform in Paris, where Black entertainers were in high demand.

Ada "Bricktop" Smith Portrait Collection, Box 1, Photographs and Prints Division, Schomburg Center for Research in Black Culture, New York Public Library, www.nypl.org.

Her fame in Paris came not as a singer but as the owner of a nightclub named after herself. She became a Charleston instructor to the rich and famous, and Bricktop's patrons included such luminaries as Fred Astaire, Jimmy Walker, Noel Coward, the Prince of Wales, Jascha Heifetz, Irving Berlin, Fats Waller, Edward G. Robinson, Gloria Swanson, Paul Robeson, Jack Johnson and T.S. Eliot (who wrote her a poem). F. Scott Fitzgerald said, "My greatest claim to fame is that I discovered Bricktop before Cole Porter," yet the songwriter Porter became Bricktop's best friend and wrote for her that morose classic "Miss Otis Regrets."[77]

Bricktop's closed in 1937, a victim of the Depression. Bricktop later owned clubs in Mexico City and Rome, but she could not recapture the magic of Bricktop's and returned to the Windy City. Bricktop, who died in 1984, performed in Chicago nightclubs into her eighties, and in 1978, the city, by mayoral proclamation, celebrated "Bricktop Day."

4

PERPETRATORS, PROSECUTORS AND PUBLIC ENEMIES

Organized Crime

He whom many fear has himself many to fear.
—Publilius Syrus (circa 85–43 BCE)

In 2015, Chicago's Field Museum announced the discovery in Zambia of a new species of pre-mammal. Because of an odd groove on the animal's upper jaw, they called it *ichibengops*, joining the Bemba word for scar (*ichibenga*) with the Greek suffix for face (*ops*)—in short, "scarface"—a name the museum directors knew would resonate with visitors, wherever they came from. "Scarface Al" Capone was and remains the most famous gangster of all time. And as *ichibengops* shows, his image endures in Chicago to this day.

Crime in Jazz Age Chicago

Most visitors to the city are undoubtedly aware that the most famous Chicagoan is not a jazz musician, or the mayor, or a sports star—he's a gangster. If you were to visit Chicago in the 1920s, could you have gotten a look at Big Al himself? The answer is yes; the mob boss was not publicity shy. Often, he could be spotted driving about the city in his armor-plated Cadillac, and tour buses regularly passed his headquarters at the Lexington Hotel.

How bad was crime in Jazz Age Chicago? The short answer: pretty bad—although that's relative. In the 1920s, the murder rate spiked to levels never

"THE MOST FAMOUS AMERICAN IN THE WORLD"
During the Jazz Age, Alphonse Capone of Chicago was not just nationally renowned, but he was also a worldwide celebrity. *From Wikimedia Commons.*

before seen in the city's history; on the other hand, it was barely half of what it would become in the 1990s. In 1924, Chicago's homicide rate was 24 percent higher than the national urban average. A year later, Greater Chicago was averaging one murder or more every day (there were also over one hundred bombings that year).[78] The *New York Times* reported that in the 1920s, Chicago experienced 43,487 violent deaths, about 10 percent of which were homicides.[79] In 1928 there were 18 murders in London, 200 in New York and 367 in Chicago, which was the smallest of the three cities.[80] Chicago's reputation was crowned with the publication in 1930 of *Chicago Gang Wars in Pictures: X Marks the Spot* by reporter Hal Andrew, which contained lurid photographs of the bloody corpses of assassinated gangsters. Also, in 1927, Chicago sociologist Frederic Thrasher published *The Gang: A Study of 1,313 Gangs in Chicago*, which analyzed how disaffected adolescents formed antisocial cliques in what the author termed *interstitial* areas—cracks in the structure of society caused by competition between contending social and ethnic groups.

In the spring of 1928, James O'Donnell of the *Chicago Tribune* wrote a front-page editorial titled "'Chicago' Word of Terror All Over World" and quoted the *Washington Post*: "The ill fame of Chicago is spreading through the world and bringing shame to Americans who wish they could be proud

THE CHICAGO GANGSTER GOES TO HOLLYWOOD
The major movie studios quickly capitalized on the nation's fascination with racketeers. Two films based on the career of Al Capone were *Little Caesar* (1931) and *Scarface* (1932) with Paul Muni, seen here in the classic gangster pose. *Author's collection.*

of that city." He told of a businessman who returned from Europe and said, "Everywhere I went, in Italy, on the Riviera, I heard evil remarks about Chicago….Judging from the reports in the papers, a European…would think every Chicagoan took his life in his hands when he stepped out of doors."[81] Stories like these rattled Chicago's business community, which worried financiers might view Chicago as an unsafe place to invest money and that tourists might hesitate to visit.

Despite the disorder, an innocent bystander's chances of being killed by a stray bullet were minuscule; as historian John J. Binder has explained, "gangland killers were fairly proficient at getting their intended victims while not hurting or killing bystanders….Residents of Cook County who were not involved with organized crime were in little danger during Prohibition, especially if they avoided…certain areas in Chicago."[82]

AL CAPONE: PUBLIC BENEFACTOR OR PUBLIC ENEMY?

Chicagoans today have mostly come to terms with their city's mobster image, offering Roaring 1920s parties, guided tours of underworld haunts and a "Gangland Chicago" exhibit at the Chicago History Museum that displays a banner with a Capone quotation: "When I sell liquor, they call it bootlegging. When my patrons serve it on silver trays on Lake Shore Drive, they call it hospitality." The claim is that Capone was merely defying a foolish alcohol prohibition law and letting honest folks relax with a drink. Many tell the stories of Capone's generosity—the free soup kitchen he ran during the Great Depression, the large donations to churches and charities. Many in Jazz Age Chicago viewed Capone as a kind of Robin Hood. One woman said, "You can say what you want about Al Capone. If people were desperate and needed help, he was there to help them." A man who worked in Capone's home said, "If there were more people like him, there wouldn't be so many poor people."[83] One could object that, aside from booze, Capone made a lot of money from illegal gambling—but isn't that a victimless crime, and aren't legal casinos now common? And as for the murders he ordered, the victims were hardly the kinds of people whose absence damaged society. As Capone himself said, "I've been spending the best years of my life as a public benefactor....My booze has been good and my games on the square."[84]

Alphonse Capone was born in Brooklyn on January 17, 1899. English was his first language, he didn't speak with an Italian accent and he didn't have a strong ethnic identity (he used to say, "I'm no Italian, I was born in Brooklyn.").[85] People have imagined he was short (similar to Napoleon, who also wasn't short), perhaps because we like to presume small size in powerful or malevolent historical figures. The producers of the Prohibition era television crime series *Boardwalk Empire*, who could have easily researched Capone's actual height, maintained this myth by casting British actor Stephen Graham, who is five feet, five inches tall, as Big Al. Similarly, in an interview that was part of a public television documentary titled *Al Capone: Icon*, a historian commented, "Capone, because of his height, fancied double-breasted suits that made him look taller and thinner." Perhaps the idea the Capone was short was reinforced by the 1931 crime film *Little Caesar*, in which the mob boss character, obviously based on Capone, was played by Edward G. Robinson, who was, like Stephen Graham, five feet, five inches tall. But in a time when the average felon, according to police records, stood five feet, three inches tall, a police record now in the Smithsonian Institution gives Capone's height as "6' 0½"." A Canadian reporter who met him in a courtroom wrote, "The Capone that I saw was over six feet tall, with shoulders wider than anybody else's in the whole courtroom."[86]

Capone's family was not poor; his father was a successful barber, and his mother sewed and took in boarders. Capone was bright; he was especially good with numbers, and in his early days in organized crime, he helped keep the books. Capone had a temper and could—and did—beat people up. But he learned to control himself, and many acquaintances were impressed by his courtesy, manners and proper English. He favored expensive suits in garish colors, like lime green and canary yellow, and a white fedora was his trademark (his associates called him "Snorky," a 1920s term for a sharp dresser). He was informed on current issues and loved opera. His morality was old-fashioned (he despised what he saw as the laxity of the Jazz Age), he was generous and loyal, he paid his aides and staff handsomely and he insisted that they act like gentlemen. According to one of his biographers, "he was sincere in how he related to people. He genuinely liked to meet people whose lives were far removed from his own closed and encapsulated criminal world."[87] He was a graceful dancer and also played golf—he wasn't particularly good, but somehow, the other players always managed to lose. Capone worked hard. Reporters who went to his office found him surrounded by a bank of ringing telephones and a swarm of assistants. Capone had nothing to do with the Mafia, as is generally believed. The Mafia was Sicilian; he was Neapolitan. In any case, Binder has calculated that only about 60 percent of Capone's gang members were Italian.[88] He was superrich—the feds estimated the take of his organization in 1927 to be over $100 million.[89] But his image as the crime boss of all Chicago is false. The city was divided into sections, with a local gang in charge of each. Capone did make alliances with several of Chicago's other gangs, but others remained enemies, which is why Capone had to travel with a cohort of bodyguards. He once said, "I haven't had any peace of mind in years. Every minute, I'm in danger of death."[90] The heart of Capone's territory was the highly lucrative Loop, the Near South Side and several suburbs, most notably Cicero. Capone's vices were wagering, whiskey and women. He lost a fortune playing craps and was a hapless bettor at the racetrack. He once totaled his gambling losses at $7.5 million and shrugged it off as the price of good times. But he wouldn't put money in the stock market, which he viewed as a "racket." He regularly went on stupefying benders. Part of his mythology is that he used drugs, especially cocaine, but the evidence of this is slight.[91] Although he married an Irish girl, Mary "Mae" Josephine Coughlin, when he was nineteen and loved her all his life, he patronized the mob's bordellos—syphilis eventually destroyed him.

Capone was barely into his teens when one Frankie Yale (Francesco Ioele) recruited him into a New York gang. Yale mentored him and put him to work as a bartender and bouncer in Coney Island. It was in Coney Island that Capone received his signature scar. He paid unwanted attention to the kid sister of Frankie Galluchio, who wielded either a knife or a broken bottle (accounts differ) and cut three slashes into Capone's face. Capone admitted that the fault was his and never sought payback. About a year later, Capone got into a fight with a member of an Irish gang and put the man into the hospital. Capone was then a target of reprisal, and Yale placed him in the care of Johnny Torrio, a Brooklyn tough guy who had moved to Chicago sometime before 1910.

The best evidence shows that Capone arrived in Chicago in 1919.[92] The top gangster of the city at the time was James "Big Jim" Colosimo, Torrio's boss. Colosimo rejected Torrio's proposal that the mob get involved in bootlegging, and Torrio felt that the chief was getting soft. Colosimo was murdered in May 1920, and although Torrio was the obvious suspect, the crime was never officially solved. Five years later, Torrio himself was the target of gunmen. He survived, but he'd had enough and left everything to Capone. Before retiring, Torrio began expanding into the suburbs. Dozens of Torrio-Capone brothels and speakeasies sprouted up outside the city. When Chicagoans elected a reform mayor, William Dever, in 1923, Torrio and Capone moved their headquarters to Cicero, where, in 1924, their thugs stole the municipal election for their puppet politicians by stuffing ballot boxes, kidnapping election officials and intimidating voters. Capone set up his office in Cicero's Hawthorne Hotel.

In Chicago, Torrio and Capone's major rival was the North Side Mob, headed by Dion O'Banion (his real first name was evidently Dean, which is what's on his tombstone, but the newspapers at the time referred to him as Dion, as do most historians). In November 1924, Torrio and Capone's hitmen slew O'Banion in his flower shop, leaving Hymie Weiss as head of the Northsiders. Weiss promptly ordered the hit that caused Torrio to leave town. On September 20, 1926, Weiss sent a parade of cars bearing gunmen into Cicero; the gunmen sprayed an estimated one thousand bullets into the Hawthorne Hotel. Capone and his men emerged unhurt, and less than three weeks later, a pair of Capone's gunmen fired ten bullets into Weiss, killing him.

Murdering Weiss didn't mean Capone was safe. His enemy Joseph Aiello offered a $5,000 reward to anyone who could bump him off, and gunmen tried to do this on four separate occasions in 1927 alone, which is why Capone bought a property on Palm Island, an enclave of Miami Beach, Florida. In 1927, Dever lost his reelection to former mayor William Hale "Big Bill" Thompson, who took the heat off of the city's gangsters. Capone transferred his command center to Chicago's Metropole Hotel, where he booked fifty rooms on two floors.

Dozens of gangsters around the country were committing the same offenses Capone did, but he was the one who became world famous. Capone made the cover of *TIME* magazine, and Hollywood filmed movies based on his life, including *Little Caesar* (1931) and *Scarface* (1932). The *New York Times* wrote that he was the best-known American in the world.[93] Capone was remarkably accessible—he enjoyed the spotlight and gave press conferences. His willingness to talk to reporters and to be photographed is what made him so well-known. Capone was to crime what Babe Ruth was to baseball and Louis Armstrong was to music—in his prominence he was the personification of the Jazz Age, the era in which mass communications created celebrity culture.

Although Capone preferred to convince people rather than use force, his dark side did surface. One of the most legendary tales about Capone tells of how, at a banquet in 1929, he bashed in the heads of three turncoats with a sawed-off baseball bat (the scene was recreated in the 1987 movie *The Untouchables*).[94] There is only one source that backs up this story, and some historians doubt that he was even at that banquet, but for biographers, the tale offers a perfect example of Capone's hot temper. The most violent crime associated with Capone was the St. Valentine's Day Massacre of 1929, in which seven members of Bugs Moran's gang were lined up against a wall in a Clark Street garage and gunned down execution-style. Capone was in Florida at the time, and his involvement was never proven.

ELIOT NESS: HERO OR HUMBUG?

Capone's most prominent nemesis was G-man Eliot Ness, the leader of the "Untouchables," made famous by TV and movies—although not everyone is an admirer. In 2014, a proposal was made to name a federal office building after Ness, but two Chicago aldermen, Edward M. Burke and James Balcer, said, "Not so fast." Burke went so far as to call the proposal "outrageous"

UNTOUCHABLE-IN-CHIEF
Although some have considered Eliot Ness overrated as a lawman, he was honest and courageous and proved to be a major nuisance to Al Capone. *From Wikimedia Commons.*

and said, "Hollywood has created an Eliot Ness myth that simply isn't true. Eliot Ness never laid eyes on Al Capone. The truth is—and we should tell the truth—Eliot Ness was a figment of Hollywood's imagination."[95] Ness did lay eyes on Capone, although not until Big Al's trial in 1931. Still, the question remains: was Eliot Ness a myth created by Hollywood, or was he a fearless G-man who took on a vicious criminal at great risk? The answer is somewhere in between.

E.C. Yellowley, the federal prohibition administrator for Illinois, believed he had to recruit a team of lawmen who hadn't been "gotten to." Eliot Ness was a Chicago boy, born on the South Side on April 19, 1902. He grew up as the straightest of straight shooters and doted on *The Adventures of Sherlock Holmes.* His mother once remarked, "I never saw a boy like him."[96] After graduating from the University of Chicago, he took a job analyzing people's credit ratings. Ness found it boring and turned to his brother-in-law, lawman Alexander Jamie, who got him a job with the Prohibition Bureau.

The government's strategy for taking down Capone had two components: one group of agents was charged with scrutinizing his income taxes, and the second had the job of destroying Capone's bootlegging operation. This second troupe was headed by Ness. Ness hardly thought Prohibition was a good idea (he was a drinker himself); it wasn't illegal liquor that troubled him but organized crime. As he explained, "I don't know how the Prohibition law was ever passed, but that wasn't my concern. What *was* my concern was the fact that an enormous industry had not gone out of business but instead had been appropriated by racketeers and hoodlums."[97]

Ness handpicked the members of his team in 1929. Its numbers fluctuated, but it usually comprised less than a dozen members. For his first target, Ness chose the suburb of Chicago Heights, a hotbed of illegal distilling. He and his men made a nighttime tour of the suburb and easily discovered no fewer than eighteen clandestine stills simply from the stench in the air. Then he borrowed a small army of Prohibition agents and closed not only every one of the stills but also the Cozy Corners Saloon, the headquarters of local crime boss Johnny Giannini.

Ness was then ready to go after Capone himself. Capone's main source of income was beer, and Big Al's henchmen went through a lot of trouble to conceal their breweries behind fake walls and the like. While spying on a speakeasy, Ness realized that because empty beer barrels had to be returned to the source, all he had to do was follow the barrels. Eventually, his men found their first brewery at 2271 Lumber Street, where they broke through the doors into a huge room that contained vats and trucks. At a Capone brewery in Cicero, Ness used a snowplow-shaped battering ram on the front of a truck to smash through its steel doors. Among the workers Ness's team arrested was Capone's master brewer, Steve Svoboda.

Ness and his men were becoming a serious concern to the Capone organization. Ness's team's cars were stolen, and his men were sometimes followed by shady figures in "pearl gray hats," but it's a myth that Capone either planned or attempted a hit on Ness. The newspapers realized what a good story Ness was, and the *Tribune* ran a large, flattering photograph of the handsome, intrepid agent.[98] It was around this time that Ness's team began to be known as the "Untouchables."[99] Fan mail poured into his office, and Ness loved the publicity.[100] His legend was beginning to take shape.

In 1931, the federal government issued two indictments against Capone. The first charged that Capone had earned over $1 million between 1924 and 1929 and hadn't paid any income taxes. The second case, based on evidence supplied by Ness, charged Capone and sixty-eight of his henchmen with five thousand counts of violations of the Prohibition laws. It was the first indictment, the income tax case, that sent Capone to prison. In that sense, Ness was not, as his later critics pointed out, the man who vanquished Capone. But he was both courageous and incorruptible, a rare combination for a Chicago lawman in the Jazz Age.

The Secret Six

The idea of a national prohibition on alcoholic beverages arose mostly from the nation's heartland—the small towns and rural regions that were home to religious zealots who feared "demon rum" and distrusted the immigrants who brought their whiskey (Irish), beer (Germans) and wine (Italians) with them (although some prominent Black Americans, such as Frederick Douglass, Booker T. Washington, Ida B. Wells, and W.E.B. Du Bois also endorsed Prohibition). So, when Prohibition went into effect, the majority of the residents of Chicago (a city with a lot of Irish, Germans and Italians) defied the law. But as the gang wars worsened, Chicago's image suffered. Outsiders began to wonder if it was safe to visit, and financiers started to ask if it was a dependable place to invest money in. Chicago's business leaders realized crime could be costing them money.

So, a small group of Chicago businessmen banded together in an organization called the "Secret Six."[101] This clandestine group, it's estimated, "contributed close to a million dollars to the Chicago Crime Commission and the IRS in the hope that they would bring down Capone."[102] The reality of the Secret Six was not a secret—the newspapers reported on the group—but their identities remained unknown, and even today, historians debate who they were. Prominent Chicago names that come up include Julius Rosenwald, Samuel Insull, Frank Loesch, Edward E. Gore, George A. Paddock, Charles Dawes, Robert McCormick, Burt A. Massee, Calvin Goddard, Henry Barrett Chamberlin, Harrison Barnard and Robert Isham Randolph, who was probably the leader. Whoever they were (and there might have been more than six), the point is that Chicago's business community was hardly complicit and passive in the face of organized crime. Like the Untouchables, they could not be bought off.

In 1919, Henry Barrett Chamberlin became the first director of the Chicago Crime Commission. When, in April 1930, the Chicago Crime Commission created a list of twenty-eight of Chicago's most dangerous gangsters, Chamberlin gave the list, which he referred to as a list of "public enemies," to *Tribune* reporter James Doherty, who ran a story with the headline, "List 28 As Public Enemies." Although the list was published alphabetically, which put Capone in the fourth spot, Big Al quickly became "public enemy no. 1."[103]

The Secret Six was behind the appointments of two key figures in Capone's conviction. First, they oversaw the appointment of George E.Q. Johnson, who went on to collect thousands of Capone-related documents as U.S. attorney for the Northern District of Illinois. Second, they engineered the hiring of federal agent Alexander Jamie, Eliot Ness's brother-in-law, who was able to construct a detailed and complicated chart of Capone's business empire, starting with what might be called a board of directors and going down to the drivers who delivered the liquor and beer.

Nevertheless, if there was one individual who was responsible for Capone's downfall, it was probably Frank J. Wilson. When President Herbert Hoover ordered Treasury Secretary Andrew Mellon to figure out a way to lock up Capone, Mellon turned to Elmer L. Irey, the head of a division of the Treasury Department called the Special Intelligence Unit (SIU). Irey assigned the case to agent Wilson. It took Wilson a year and a half of relentless inquiry, but he unearthed papers that showed how Capone had been given a cut of the income earned by the Chicago Mob. Capone had not paid income tax on this money, and on October 24, 1931, he received a sentence of eleven years' imprisonment, $50,000 in fines and $30,000 in court costs. Capone did his time, first in Atlanta and then on the "Rock"—Alcatraz Prison in San Francisco Bay. When he was released in November 1939, he went straight into a hospital. His progressive syphilis had rendered the once-ferocious gang boss harmless. His mental age was assessed at around seven or ten (on good days, fourteen). He comfortably lived out his days in Florida, lapsing in and out of lucidity, until he died on January 25, 1947. The Secret Six, having achieved their major objective, went out of business in early 1933.[104]

The Verdict of History

When Capone was pressed about his criminal activities, he always mentioned just two—alcohol and gambling, both of which are now legal and not controversial. But Capone's empire also included dozens of brothels. A Cicero journalist named Robert St. John exposed the conditions in these places and revealed how the "women" were mostly country girls lured to the city with the promise of decent jobs and then terrorized and sold like slaves. For his pains, St. John was beaten up by four of Capone's men.[105] Also, the common view that Chicago's assassins murdered only one another is incorrect; gangsters killed eighteen law enforcement officials in Jazz Age Chicago.[106] Further, the evidence is strong that the Torrio-Capone Gang "was behind the dope trade in Chicago during Prohibition."[107] Chicago had a lively drug scene in the Jazz Age—the preferred narcotics being morphine, cocaine and opium, which was known as "hop"—and at the time, *New Republic* magazine reported that Capone "has been closely allied with the most loathsome of all traffics, that in habit-forming drugs."[108] Finally, Capone controlled the Mob that became known as the "Chicago Outfit," a group that plagued honest businesses for decades to come.

By the late 1920s, Capone estimated that Prohibition would not survive more than four or five more years, and consequently, he got into labor racketeering. Taking control of labor unions paid off in several ways: he could steal from the pension funds, he could accept bribes from employers for calling off a strike and he could, as one Capone ally put it, "grab the treasuries."[109] Eventually, Capone controlled the plumbers', sanitation workers', street cleaners', steamfitters' and construction workers' unions and no fewer than thirty-three unions related to transportation.[110] Muscling in on legitimate businesses also proved to be lucrative. If, say, he could set the prices for every dry cleaner in the city, he could charge whatever he wanted and keep a percentage of the profits, and it was reported that the price of cleaning a suit went from $1.25 to $1.75.[111] In 1929, the Employees' Association of Chicago counted ninety-one businesses that had been infiltrated by the mob. According to historian Gerald Leinwand, the Chicago industries "especially prone to the protection racket" included "laundry cleaning and dyeing, linen supply, carbonated beverages, barbers, bakers, coal, kosher meats, building material, paving, excavating, flour, tobacco, beauty culture, roofing material, municipal workers, garages, dairy products, demolition, perishable produce, long-distance hauling, distribution of ice cream, furniture storage, ash and garbage removal, machinery moving, railway express, lumber, florists, baggage delivery, janitors, commercial window washers, oil wagons drivers, electrotyping, and motion picture operators."[112] To enforce this control, Capone's men bombed stores and factories, hijacked trucks, poured acid on the clothes in laundries and beat up or murdered owners and employees.[113] Candy vendors who refused to join the Capone-controlled Candy Jobbers Association were bombed, beaten and stabbed.[114] It was a kind of racketeering tax on consumers—the Chicago Crime Commission estimated it to be $200 million a year.[115] Sucking that kind of money out of ordinary working folk hardly qualifies one as a public benefactor.

It wouldn't be a stretch to claim that Al Capone played a part in making Chicago the crucible of modern America. The eminent American sociologist Robert K. Merton (1910–2003) considered Capone a true "innovator." In the late 1930s, Merton developed what sociologists term *strain theory*, which analyzes the stresses that arise when defined goals exist without the means to achieve them—whether or not these goals are legitimate. These stresses can foster "antisocial behavior," and Merton went on to argue that innovation is one of the four deviant activities that can result (the others are ritualism, retreatism and rebellion). Merton placed Capone into the innovation category and wrote, "Al Capone represents the triumph of amoral intelligence over morally prescribed 'failure' when the channels of vertical mobility are closed or narrowed in a society that places a high premium on economic affluence and social ascent for all its members."[116] It's not something to be proud of, but modern organized crime began in Jazz Age Chicago.

INTERLUDE: GANGSTER FUNERALS

In the Jazz Age, gangster funerals were regular occurrences, but Chicago had a reputation for staging the gaudiest, most elaborate last rites for racketeers. One of the grandest was that of Dean, or Dion, O'Banion, the head of the North Side Gang who was gunned down by Al Capone's hitmen on November 10, 1924.

The streets surrounding the chapel that held the wake were jammed with crowds for blocks, while hundreds gazed on from rooftops and windows. Fifty police officers cleared the way for the cortege as twenty-six truckloads of flowers accompanied the hearse to Mount Carmel Cemetery, where thousands of mourners awaited the $10,000 silver casket. The cost of the funeral was estimated to be $100,000, although the flowers were presumably bought at a discount because O'Banion's official trade was as a florist. A prominent Chicago minister lamented that "a man said to have been implicated in twenty-five murders" was "buried with the pomp and ceremony of a king."[117]

Chicago Italians' pride wouldn't let them be outdone by the Irish. Only six months later, the slain Sicilian racketeer Angelo Genna was laid to rest. The Gennas blamed O'Banion's North Side successor and deliberately bought an even more costly coffin (the slaying was probably Capone's work). Again, police barricaded the crowded street. A parade of trucks hauled in the flowers—roses, pinks, peonies, lilies—which were then ferried to the cemetery in thirty-one limousines. The *Chicago Tribune* observed that if O'Banion had set the "yardstick" for opulent funerals, "Angelo's pageant stood the test and came out on top."[118]

5

ZIGZAGS, BUNGALOWS AND STREAMLINING

BUILDING A CITY MODERNE

For Chicagoans and visitors alike, the golden age of the city's architecture remains the 1890s, when Chicago's visionary designers developed the skyscraper. The city's two most prominent architects were Daniel Burnham and Louis Sullivan. In the 1890s, the third member of Chicago's triumvirate, Frank Lloyd Wright, was beginning his ascent, although by the Jazz Age, he was generally acknowledged to be America's greatest architect.

And yet, despite the valorization of the 1890s, unappreciated developments occurred in the 1920s. Chicago reinvented the skyscraper, and the aesthetic was no longer the Classical Revival, Beaux-Arts School of Burnham and the White City—it was Art Deco or "jazz moderne," as it was often called at the time. Deco's zigzags and stylized abstractions made critics think of the hot, new music, of which Chicago was the capital.

A NEW GENERATION OF SKYSCRAPERS

Chicago architecture in the Jazz Age has a special position in American architectural history. First, the pace of construction in the city in the 1920s was prodigious. Second, the tall buildings represented a significant rethinking of the look and purpose of the skyscraper, as well as a rejection of earlier ideals of city planning. Third, the period serves as a case study in shifting tastes—a recognition that building styles go in and out of favor, a constant factor in cultural history that has real consequences. Both Chicagoans and visitors might be surprised to discover how much Art Deco architecture Chicago possesses. Finally, surveying Chicago in the Jazz Age enables us to rescue one of the most neglected aspects of historic construction—domestic architecture.

Two major developments put an end to the golden age of 1890s skyscrapers: the decade brought a major depression, which halted investment for years, and in 1893, the city put a height limit on new buildings. This was at a time when New York skyscrapers were soaring. Chicagoans began feeling embarrassed. Their city had practically invented the skyscraper, and it was then being outclassed by Manhattan. And it wasn't just pride that was at stake. Earle Shultz, the president of the National Association of Building Owners and Managers, complained that Chicago's height restrictions had "crippled" the city's economic growth.[119]

By the early 1920s, Chicago's builders had found a loophole. The building code allowed the construction of "towers, domes, and spires" on roofs so long as they remained within certain size restrictions. The first Jazz Age skyscraper to take advantage of this loophole was the Wrigley Building (1921), which, at 398 feet, became Chicago's tallest building. It was followed two years later by the Chicago Temple (1923), which was built by the Methodist Church and had a spire that rose 568 feet above the pavement.

In 1923, the city adopted a "setback ordinance" that allowed taller skyscrapers if their profiles were "set back" in stages as they rose. In effect, there was no longer a height restriction. Soon, Chicago boasted the London Guarantee Building, the Straus Building and the Jewelers Building, all in the neoclassical, Beaux-Arts style of Burnham's White City.

The Tribune Tower

No important urban building gets constructed today unless several architectural firms contend for the job, and sometimes, these competitions stir a great deal of commentary. But the most legendary of all architectural competitions took place in Chicago during the Jazz Age. On June 10, 1922, the *Chicago Tribune*, which was marking its seventy-fifth anniversary, announced that it was erecting a great new building to house the "world's greatest newspaper."[120] Architects from all over the world were invited to send in designs, and the prize money would total $100,000. Not only did the great competition that ensued give Chicago an impressive new tower,

"TOWERING AND MILITANT"
In 1922, the *Chicago Tribune* held a worldwide competition for the design of a skyscraper. The entries constitute a survey of skyscraper architecture from the 1890s to the 1950s. The winning design, inspired by the Gothic Revival, was provided by Howells and Hood of New York. *Author's collection.*

but, as the architecture historian Joanna Merwood-Salisbury has written, it "inaugurated a third generation of Chicago skyscrapers."[121]

The *Tribune* did not signal what kind of skyscraper the owners preferred, but it strongly suggested that modernism was not what they had in mind. For weeks, the paper published pictures of famous structures—the Pantheon, St. Peter's Basilica in Rome and various European cathedrals—leaving readers to decide which might serve as a model. The *Tribune's* directors clearly believed that the new skyscraper would be a link in a chain of famous buildings stretching back to antiquity.

The deadline for submissions was noon on November 1, 1922, although the *Tribune* granted a "grace period" of thirty days for entries coming from far away. The number of designs eventually received was 263, 59 of which came in too late. The names of the architects were not revealed; the drawings were identified only by a number. Few of the designs were what would qualify today as "modern." Most of them featured decorated nonfunctional tops—crowns, domes, spires, colossal statues and so on. The *Tribune* described the entries as a mix of "the noble and the banal, the stately and the sensational, the chaste and bizarre, the practical and the grotesque."[122] A few European designs were imaginatively modern and would not look out of place alongside the glass towers of the 1950s. The jury pored over them until November 13, when they cast their first ballot, which favored three entries—those by Howells and Hood of New York, Holabird and Roche of Chicago and Frederick Adams of Kansas City. The advisory committee then added nine more, all of them from the United States.

But minutes before the grace period expired, an unexpected package arrived. The *Tribune* reported:

> *An eleventh-hour entry from Europe caused a sensation yesterday.… Something colossal from across the seas was cleared through the customs at noon. Telephones and automobiles got into action, and the advisory committee of city officials and citizens—who thought on Wednesday of last week that their work was done—hurriedly reassembled to consider the new entry.…The latest arrival—its heavy wrappings strewn over the floor—smote them with its message of silent majesty from a distance of fifty feet.*[123]

The advisory committee quickly recommended the design be given "most favorable consideration."[124] Entry 187 was from Finland; the architect was Eliel Saarinen. A stunning, soaring design, it was "relatively unadorned, with

"SOMETHING
COLOSSAL FROM
ACROSS THE SEAS"
Eliel Saarinen's
design for the
Tribune Tower
finished in second
place, but it turned
out to be a spur
for the Art Deco
movement, as
architects emulated
its style and
audacity. *Courtesy of
the Library of Congress.*

a series of narrow stone piers angling skyward like lightning bolts."[125] It was, however, just outside the jury's comfort zone; they couldn't deny its power but awarded it second prize. The victorious entry from John Mead Howells and Raymond Hood was an extravagant riff on the flamboyant French Gothic style, modeled on the Tour de Beurre (1506) at the cathedral of Rouen. The *Tribune* described the design as "towering and militant" and said it would be "an ornament and an inspiration to the city we love."[126]

Saarinen's proposal, however, became surprisingly influential. Only five years after the contest, architecture critic Thomas Tallmadge wrote that in its design "lay the solution of the skyscraper, a veritable philosopher's stone that would transmute the dross of eclecticism into the gold of new architecture."[127] The first skyscraper in Chicago that showed the impact of Saarinen's design was 333 North Michigan Avenue (1928) by Holabird and Root, which is considered Chicago's first Art Deco tower. Even Hood and Howells were to fall under Saarinen's spell. Hood's American Radiator Building in New York was inspired by the Finnish master, as was Howells's Panhellic Tower (now New York's Beekman Tower). Alfred Finn's Gulf Building in Houston (1929) is a virtual lookalike. The lure of the design still resonated in 1990, when Cesar Pelli's skyscraper at 181 West Madison Street in Chicago was built. Its similarity to Saarinen's model is unmistakable.[128] A building that was never constructed became more influential than the hundreds that were.

ART DECO CHICAGO

Tours of Chicago's Jazz Age skyscrapers are popular because the buildings are in the Art Deco style, which was once considered kitsch but is now eminently fashionable. But before there were Art Deco skyscrapers, there were Art Deco chairs, jewelry pieces, fabrics and ceramics.

The term *Art Deco* comes from a historic exhibition in Paris in 1925 called *L'Exposition internationale des arts decoratifs et industriels moderne* ("arts decoratifs" became "art deco"). As discussed in the introduction of this book, "Making America Modern," the preferred way to describe objects created in the new style at the time was "moderne" or "modern" or even "jazz moderne." Twenty-one countries were represented in the Parisian show, which highlighted decorative objects, especially luxury goods, although paintings, furniture, textiles and architecture were also included. There, many visitors got their first look at the motifs that would come to characterize Art Deco—

geometric patterns, zigzags, lightning bolts, chevrons, sunbursts, overlapping arches, Aztec and Egyptian designs, abstracted animal forms (especially does) and stylized flower bouquets, along with the influences of cubism, constructivism and futurism, as well as African art.

In the United States, the initial impact of the Paris exhibit was felt in the area of home furnishings and luxury objects, and Chicagoans rapidly adopted the trend. In June 1925, while the Paris exposition was still going on, the John A. Colby Furniture Store was showing what it called an "Exposition Spéciale des Meubles Modernes." The display featured "exact duplicates" of objects shown in Paris, and its advertisement stated, "No movement in art in nearly two centuries has created so much interest as the 'moderne' in furniture."[129] Arthur Fraser, a longtime manager of the Window Display Department at Marshall Field's Department Store, grew keen on Art Deco, and actual objects that had been displayed in the exposition were first seen in Chicago in the windows at Field's. Then in 1926, a tour displaying some four hundred objects that had been shown in Paris made the rounds, and the Art Institute of Chicago was one of the venues included.[130] The following year, at Field's, Fraser mounted a window display of furniture based on abstract art. Also, two young Chicago architects and designers, Robert Switzer and Harold O. Warner, opened a store, Secession Ltd., which was the first in the Windy City to sell nothing but moderne furniture, glass, fabrics, pottery and so on imported from Europe. After their wares swiftly sold out, the pair began designing modern furniture themselves, hiring local cabinetmakers to do the work.[131]

In the 1930s, Art Deco morphed into a less florid, less geometric style when designers incorporated the popular vogue for "streamlining"—from which they adapted the ubiquitous motif of horizontal parallel lines, usually three, which were nicknamed "speed stripes."[132] Whereas the first wave of Art Deco was about elegance, romance and fine materials, the second was more centered on speed and machinery—streamlining became especially characteristic of automobiles, locomotives, household items and architectural touches, like round windows and glass brick.[133] One of the most popular sights at Chicago's Century of Progress Exposition of 1933–34 was the *Zephyr*, a sleek, stainless steel, diesel-powered locomotive created by the Chicago-based Chicago, Burlington & Quincy Railroad. It inspired American designers to apply the streamlined style to all manner of objects, a trend that was one of Chicago's key contributions to modernism. It was axiomatic to the new designers that streamlining led to functionality, which led to beauty. And with streamlined modernity, beautiful objects were no longer only available to the elite. In 1934, the *Chicago Tribune* published a large, illustrated feature article titled "Whole World Awheel Goes Streamline." It featured photographs of sleek racecars, airplanes, automobiles, locomotives and railroad passenger cars. According to the author of the article, "When all is said and done, streamlining is the main peg upon which engineers are hanging hopes for the future of transportation."[134] According to art historian Jeffery T. Meikle, "Within a few years streamlining spread from planes, cars, and trains to non-moving artefacts at every scale—from radios and vacuum cleaners to store fronts and restaurant interiors. Streamlining swept past other expressions of modernity with an irresistible metaphoric power."[135] Horticulturists produced "streamlined plants"—one company, for example, developed a streamlined potato (no "deep eyes"). And even psychologists got in on the trend; in 1936, educational theorist James Mursell published a self-help book titled *Streamline Your Mind*.

Until recently, Chicago's position at the pinnacle of twentieth-century American design was little known. But the secret is out. Art historian Robert Bruegmann, for example, has recently asserted that Chicago was "certainly one of the country's most important centers for commissioning, building, manufacturing and distributing Art Deco design."[136] One key component of the city's powerful influence was the presence of many factories that turned out moderne products that were then shipped across the United States by way of the city's large railroad network. Another was the location in the Windy City of Montgomery Ward and Sears & Roebuck, the two largest catalog retailers in the country. These companies sold Chicago-made Art Deco products across the nation, and many were fashioned from novel materials like aluminum, chrome and Bakelite, which were ideal for the curvilinear, streamlined style. For example, Sears hired Raymond Loewy, one of the best-known designers of the period, to design its celebrated Coldspot refrigerator, while in 1931, Montgomery Ward opened a special Bureau of Design to oversee a modernization of its products. The head of this office was the extraordinary Anne Swainson (1888–1955), a forgotten giant of streamlined modernism. Born in Missouri, she studied at the University of Missouri, Columbia Teachers College and the University of Chicago and became an expert on textiles before branching out into industrial design in general. In 1932, she was hired by Montgomery Ward, which was struggling with the effects of the Great Depression. Although Swainson designed some objects herself, she assembled a staff of artists and engineers to produce most of the others and revolutionized both the Ward's catalog and its products, which were then smartly moderne (and the sales of which pulled Ward's out of the red).[137] Chicago was also home to *Popular Mechanics* magazine, whose vividly colored covers and high-tech articles displayed the wonders of technology to both men and women readers.

According to architecture historian Pauline Saliga, "Some types of Chicago design, such as furniture development and manufacture, have always had a national impact, and the city dominated that industry from the late nineteenth century to the 1950s." In 1920, there were about 250 furniture factories in Chicago, and they were making 20 percent of the furniture produced in the United States. After 1925, the work of Chicago's designers took on a decidedly modern look, and several prominent Chicago architects entered the field of furniture design.[138] Finally, as architecture historian Jonathan Mekinda, who was cited in the introduction, has explained, "Between 1910 and 1950, as companies in the city designed, manufactured and distributed a vast range of products and goods that effectively defined the Machine Age, Chicago played a central role in making America modern."[139] Thanks to Chicago designers, what was good for skyscrapers and locomotives was also good for the home.

Probably the most original Chicago Art Deco designer was the Swiss-born Abel Marius Faidy (1894–1965), who came to the Windy City in 1918. Advertising himself as an "exponent of the Paris and Viennese School of Modernistic Decorative and Practical Creations in Home Interior Treatments, Furniture, Color Schemes and Lighting Problems," he designed interiors for offices, showrooms and so on.[140] For the Hotel Sherman, he created a soda fountain called the Aeroplane Room, which, with its sleek curved lines, its moderne lettering, its streamlining and its tubular counter stools, is nearly the perfect image of what people envision when they think of an Art Deco interior. His innovative furniture has been termed "zigzag modern."[141] For the art patrons Charles and Ruth Singletary, Faidy produced a striking fourteen-piece furniture suite; the dining room chairs and settee evoke the cutbacks of Chicago's Art Deco skyscrapers. As historian Sharon Darling has put it, "Perhaps Faidy…believed that the lines of the furniture in a modern apartment should harmonize with the cityscape visible through its windows."[142] The impact of skyscrapers on interior design was recognized at the time; in 1929, Mildred May Osgood, a student at the University of Chicago, completed a master's thesis titled "The Influence of the Skyscraper Upon Modern Decorative Arts."

In 1929, the Chicago-area W.H. Howell Co. began manufacturing chrome-plated tubular steel frames (called "Chromesteel") that incorporated the zigzag skyscraper style. Two years later, Howell's Moderne Furniture

PRACTICALLY PURE DECO
With its stylishly "moderne" font; sleek, curved lines; streamlining; and tubular counter stools, Abel Faidy's Aeroplane Room hits just about every note of an archetypal Art Deco structure. *Courtesy of the Chicago History Museum, Heinrich-Blessing Collection, HB-01383.*

Division began manufacturing tubular metal furniture, a touchstone progressive style of the Jazz Age. These Howell chairs and couches "can probably be regarded as the important beginnings for tubular steel furniture in America."[143] The Howell designs were especially prominent at the Century of Progress Exposition in Chicago, from which their popularity was spread nationwide.

The Howell chairs were only one of the many examples of modern design that this fair, held to commemorate the centennial of Chicago's incorporation as a town, placed before the eyes of millions of visitors. One and a half million people, for example, passed through the Home and Industrial Arts Exhibit in the first season, and there, they experienced "the potential of advances in science and technology in a way that was so tangibly relevant to their daily lives."[144] The most exciting example of what the future promised for the middle-class homeowner was to be found in the House of Tomorrow, the work of another nearly forgotten Chicago designer, George Frederick Keck (1895–1980). This twelve-sided, three-floored domicile, built around a central core containing a stairwell, featured both air conditioning and solar heating and was filled with all manner of labor-saving appliances and streamlined-styled furniture, including some from Howell. The ground floor boasted not only an automobile garage but also an airplane hangar. (Jazz Age visionaries expected that one day, private planes would be nearly as common as private automobiles.)

Finally, few things speak of Art Deco more than the unmistakable lettering used in advertising and posters of the era, and another easily overlooked and unappreciated aspect of Chicago's pioneering role in forging modernism is in the area of printing typefaces, or fonts. In the late 1920s, the Ludlow Typograph Company of Chicago became the leading American designer of characteristic Art Deco lettering. The firm employed two especially noteworthy designers: Douglas C. McMurtrie and Robert Hunter Middleton. Three of their most successful moderne typefaces were Ultra-Modern, Karnak and Stellar.[145]

In 1928, WillElla De Campi of the *Chicago Tribune* wrote, "Art modern is receiving a great deal of notice at the present time in important exhibitions throughout the country. The interest everywhere manifested in these shows is strongly indicative of a general enthusiasm and desire for 'something new.'"[146] A year later, Chicago's American Furniture Mart hosted a huge special exhibit of the latest styles. Reviewing the show, Kathleen M'Laughlin of the *Tribune* wrote, "If it's extreme and grotesque, it's modernistic; if it's a bit less radical but still somewhat startling to live with, it's moderne; but if it exploits the most recent and restrained evolution of the style, displayed most often

TUBES "MODERNE"
In 1931, the Chicago-area W.H. Howell Co. began making tubular metal furniture, a hallmark futuristic style of the Jazz Age. Vienna-born Wolfgang Hoffman designed this serving cart for the firm's "Moderne Furniture." *Courtesy of the Chicago History Museum, ICHi-170354.*

FONTS FOR THE FUTURE
During the Jazz Age, the Ludlow Typograph Company of Chicago was the leading American designer of characteristic Art Deco lettering. Karnak was one of its most successful "moderne" typefaces. *Author's collection.*

in solarium and garden furniture, it deserves the term *modern*."[147] When reporter John Drury visited Marshall Field's around 1927, he was "shown a room furnished in futuristic art.…Curious geometrical furniture and odd color arrangements met our eyes. Pointing to a book-case of squares and rectangles, without any apparent sense of proportion about it, the guide said: 'If you'll narrow your eyes in glancing at it, the book-case will give you the illusion of a skyscraper. That is the aim of ultra-modern, or futuristic, art—to break away from historical backgrounds and instead reflect the modern age of skyscrapers and geometry.'"[148]

As Art Deco recedes into the past, critics, as well as the general public, frequently disheartened by the questionable edifices of contemporary architecture, are coming to appreciate that Art Deco was, in the words of journalists Brianna Rennix and Nathan J. Robinson, "the last truly impressive movement in architecture."[149] Not only that, but, as historian Mike Hope has expressed it, "Art Deco architecture as developed in America became the first true influential American style that ultimately was exported around the world."[150] Chicago has at least a dozen skyscrapers, along with scores of smaller buildings, that qualify as Art Deco. As mentioned, the first Art Deco building to reflect the influence of Saarinen's design for the Tribune Tower in Chicago was 333 North Michigan Avenue, where the Art Deco aesthetic is seen in its chamfered, or beveled, corners and what has been called its "ziggurat profile." The building is also notable for its series of six large bas-reliefs on the fifth floor by sculptor Fred M. Torrey, which depict scenes of early Chicago—incorporating sculpture into buildings' façades became a favorite Art Deco device. The Chicago firm Holabird and Root quickly established itself as a master of Art Deco architecture. Its Chicago Motor Club (1928) stands out for both its exterior elegance and its interior decoration. When it was converted into a hotel in 2015, Blair Kamin, an architecture critic for the *Chicago Tribune*, wrote, "All of Art Deco's defining characteristics are compressed into this fabulous, 15-story package.…A trim silhouette with strong vertical lines; stylish geometric decoration; and a

117—Palmolive Building,
by Night, Chicago

© CURT TEICH & CO., INC.

"SILVER TOWER"
The imposing Palmolive
Building, by Holabird and
Root, was once crowned
by an intense rotating
beacon that was meant to
guide airplanes to Midway
Airport. *Author's collection.*

superb integration of art and architecture, especially in the lobby....Thank goodness such irreplaceable visual richness is still with us."[151] Holabird & Root's Palmolive Building (1929), which became known as "the silver tower," uses both horizontal and vertical setbacks—an innovation that was soon adopted in other Art Deco skyscrapers.[152] Three other Chicago Art Deco beauties from Holabird & Root are the Chicago Daily News Building (1929, now Riverside Plaza), the Buckingham Building (1930) and the LaSalle-Wacker Building (1930). The firm followed these with the towering Board of Trade Building (1930), which was the tallest building in Chicago until 1965. The team also built two spectacular structures for Chicago's Century of Progress Exposition: the flashy, modernistic Chrysler Building and the enormous and ingenious Travel and Transport Building.[153]

ART DECO WRIT LARGE
When Chicago's Merchandise Mart opened in 1930, it was the largest building in the world. Today, it is considered an Art Deco treasure, especially for its interior design. *Author's collection.*

GIANT OF MUSIC
Chicago's Civic Opera House
(1929) was the most technically
advanced opera house of its
time. To many observers, the
Art Deco colossus, as seen from
across the river, resembled a
giant armchair. *Author's collection.*

One of Chicago's finest Art Deco buildings is not exactly a skyscraper. Although it's tall (340 feet, twenty-five stories), it's also two blocks wide. When it opened in 1930, it was, at 4 million square feet, the largest building in the world. According to the architecture historian Jay Pridmore, the Merchandise Mart defines "as few buildings could, the streamlined Art Deco style that symbolized the prosperous, stylish decade in which it was designed."[154] The Merchandise Mart was built over a railyard and thus was one of the first buildings to employ the concept of "air rights."[155] The interior is where much of the building's finest Art Deco touches can be seen—the terrazzo floors, sleek lines, streamlined contours, square-fluted piers and the murals by Jules Guérin. To appreciate a building's art moderne styling, a visitor needs to scrutinize not just the building's profile but also its exterior decoration and interior styling. One critic has commented that it's not the exterior form of the skyscraper that makes it Art Deco but the ornamental decoration.[156] The use of beautiful ornamentation in buildings pretty much ended after the Art Deco era, a development mourned by critics of contemporary architecture.[157]

The Merchandise Mart was designed by the Chicago firm Graham, Anderson, Probst and White (GAPW), whose flair for Art Deco is also displayed in the Shedd Aquarium and the Civic Opera House.[158] Of the opera house, opera historian Robert C. Marsh has said, "If you like art of the 1920s…the building would never fail to impress."[159] The opera house was as innovative and moderne as anything else in Jazz Age Chicago. The stage was a copious 120 feet wide, and the spacious orchestra pit could be raised and lowered. The building contained an enormous costume department and a room with hundreds of models for stage sets. Herbert M. Johnson, the manager of the opera house, boasted that the scenery department had "three huge floors, seventy feet by fifty feet, on which the canvas is laid flat and painted."[160] *Popular Mechanics* magazine published a lavishly colored article on the technical wonders of the new house entitled "The Magic Wand of the Opera."

MODERNISM FOR THE MIDDLE CLASS

Although Chicago's Art Deco skyscrapers, with their ziggurat profiles and beveled corners, epitomized modernity in the Jazz Age, another type of Chicago building brought Art Deco modernity much more directly into people's lives. It was in these structures that Chicago made America modern in a personal, firsthand way.

When we think of a city, we think of big buildings, but that was not where most Jazz Age Chicagoans lived. In 1923, Chicago had 135,840 single-family houses, 96,500 two-family houses and 37,639 apartment houses.[161] Before the Roaring Twenties, during World War I, Chicago's working-class families were usually squeezed into multiple-family dwellings, often an older one-family house that had been divided into apartments or a dark frame cottage that had been pushed to the back of a lot to make room for a larger building out front. Many neighborhoods had few gardens or backyards, and adjectives like *bleak* and *dilapidated* were used to describe these districts. Gas, electricity and indoor plumbing were not unheard of in these areas but were expensive and out of reach for most. By 1930, however, an innovative style of housing—the "bungalow"—swept across Chicago the way the Great Fire once had.

After World War I, the newspapers were full of laments about the housing shortage and spike in rents in Chicago. But as prosperity returned, developers snapped up undeveloped lots and put up bungalows by the thousands.[162] In the 1920s, rapid growth occurred in the outer neighborhoods and near

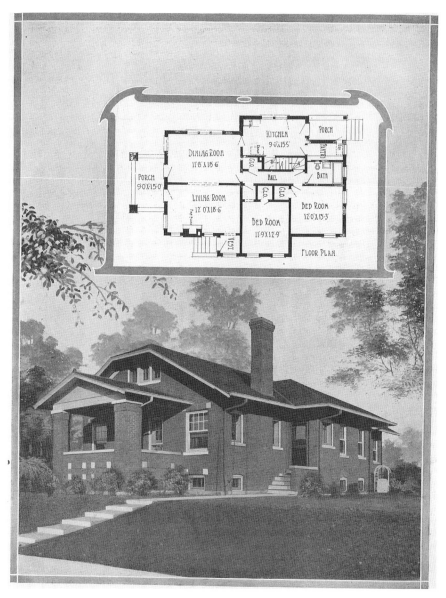

MODERNITY FOR THE MASSES
The bungalow might seem quaint today, but in its time, it was viewed as a trailblazing innovation that incorporated the best of new technology and "moderne" stylings. Some eighty thousand bungalows were built in Chicago during the Jazz Age. *From Wikimedia Commons.*

suburbs, and an estimated 100,000 bungalows were built in Chicago's nearest suburbs and in some unincorporated sections of Cook County.[163] Suburban Berwyn, for example, was said to be the fastest-growing city in the nation, with a population that grew by more than 200 percent in the 1920s.[164] By 1930, 1 out of every 4 houses in Chicago was less than ten years old.[165] The bungalow belt cut a C-shaped swath around Chicago's North, West, and South Sides, and the inner neighborhoods spilled over into adjacent suburbs, such as Berwyn and Cicero, as well as into Indiana.

In its heyday the bungalow was considered revolutionary and roomy. Its designers adopted the values of the earlier American Arts and Crafts movement, which promoted the idea that principles of creative design, based on simplicity and craftwork and the use of attractive and durable materials, could be applied to the environment of the working class. Thus, the interiors of these one-and-a-half-story bungalows boasted quality elements—fireplaces, decorative glass, archways, hardwood floors and trim, built-in bookcases and durable, hygienic, glazed tiles and mosaics on walls and floors in kitchens and bathrooms. All of the exterior walls were made of long-lasting and fireproof solid brick, often with carved stone trim. Some design features (wide eaves, an overhanging horizontal roof line, artistic glass) were adapted from Chicago's own Prairie School of architecture, which had originated with Frank Lloyd Wright.

The Historic Chicago Bungalow Association lists eight characteristics of Chicago bungalows: built between 1910 and 1940; one and a half stories high; a rectangular shape, narrow at front and back and long on the sides; an offset front entrance or a side entrance; generous windows; a full basement; face brick with stone trim; and a low, pitched roof with an overhang. The bungalows were at least 26 feet wide, which meant that lots were at least 30 feet wide, as opposed to the 20 feet allotted for the earlier workingmen's cottages. The standard bungalow had five primary rooms on the first floor; the second floor was unfinished but offered the possibility of adding two more rooms. Bungalows ranged in size from about 1,200 to 2,400 square feet. This might seem small today, but it could mean a bedroom for each child and a separate dining room—true luxuries for working-class families.

The modernity of the bungalow depended—to a great extent—on electricity. In the 1920s, the residential use of electricity more than tripled, and bungalow owners could enjoy an electric range, refrigerator and dishwasher; 80 percent of bungalow owners had electric irons and more than a third had vacuum cleaners, clothes washers, toasters and fans. In addition to electricity, natural gas also became common in the new bungalows.

The designs of appliances followed the popular "streamlining" aesthetic and brought the moderne stylings of Art Deco into middle-class homes; this all helped create the world's first consumer economy.[166] According to William E. Meehan Jr., a historian of industrial design, Chicago, "more than any other city, became the center of invention for the kitchen."[167] Some examples of Art Deco–styled appliances from Chicago include Hotpoint toasters, Streamliner radios, electric fans from the Edgar T. Ward Company, "combined" telephones from the Automatic Electric Company (the sender and receiver were at the ends of a single piece held in one hand), and Hamilton electric calendar clocks, all of which are now highly collectible.[168] In 1930, Chicago-based Sunbeam Products introduced the Mixmaster, one of the most enduring kitchen appliances. Its ingenious interlocking beaters, the inspiration of a Swedish immigrant designer named Ivar Jepson, made the device an immediate success. And some bungalow dwellers surely bought the Sunbeam chrome and Bakelite coffee set that are featured in this book's opening. As for modern radios, several Chicago firms led the way in their design. The Operadio Corporation, founded in 1922, produced what most historians agree was the first portable radio, and in 1930, Chicago's Galvin Manufacturing Corporation introduced the Motorola radio, which was so successful, the company eventually changed its name to Motorola (also in 1930, Galvin unveiled the first practical car radio). The Zenith Radio Corporation had a massive manufacturing facility on South Iron Street, where the company turned out many Art Deco–styled radios. Finally, in 1933, the huge Chicago-based bicycle maker Schwinn caught the streamlining bug and began turning out bicycles influenced by the aesthetic qualities of modern locomotives and automobiles.

In the 1920s, builders recommended including twenty-five electrical outlets in every home—more than two per room. As early as 1912, the famous inventor Thomas Edison predicted, "The housewife of the future will be neither a slave to servants nor herself a drudge. She will give less attention to the home, because the home will need less; she will be rather a domestic engineer than a domestic laborer, with the greatest of all handmaidens, electricity, at her service."[169] Accordingly, the labor-saving features of the modern bungalow were marketed as blessings for wives and mothers. By the time Edison made his statement, the number of hours devoted to housework per week began its century-long plunge from around sixty to the mid-twenties, where it is today.[170] Finally, telephone usage expanded 70 percent between 1924 and 1929.[171]

DECO IN THE KITCHEN
Chicago manufacturers
led the way in bringing
"moderne" designs to
the home. This gazelle-
themed toaster, designed
by Raymond E. Patten
for Hotpoint, is a striking
example. *Courtesy of the
Chicago Museum of Science
and Industry.*

In Chicago, bungalow prices ranged from $2,500 to $10,000 ($37,500 to $150,000 in today's currency). Credit was available from several sources, and developers and builders partnered with banks and mortgage brokers. Meanwhile, many ethnic communities had their own building and loan associations. It was possible for a buyer to move into a new bungalow with $100 down and a monthly mortgage payment of $25 plus interest.[172] Even at these prices, bungalows were generally not in the reach of the poor—few were built in underserved Black communities—but they were in the price range of a fireman, teacher or factory hand at the upper range of the pay scale. One of the key features of the bungalow boom was that it brought homeownership to middle-class and working-class buyers who formerly didn't have the means. Although the cost of living rose by 64 percent from 1914 to 1927, wages went up by 134 percent.[173] Then women could also contribute to the household income—a paper published in 1929 by the Department of Labor showed that in 1920, nearly one out of four women who were "gainfully employed" were married. As the author of the paper put it, "women's contribution to family support is considerable."[174] As historian Joseph Bigott has expressed it, "most people who purchased bungalows in the 1920s bought structures larger and more complex than the houses in which they were born. To suggest otherwise fails to recognize the effects of economic abundance and social mobility in the twentieth century."[175]

Today, one out of every three single-family homes in Chicago is a bungalow. In 2000, the city, along with the Chicago Architecture Foundation and the Chicago Historic Bungalow Association, launched the Historic Chicago Bungalow Initiative, a marketing, educational and financial project meant to publicize and protect the Chicago bungalow. Today, nearly a dozen areas are designated as bungalow historic districts, including Falconer, Wrightwood, Talman West Ridge and Rogers Park Manor. They offer inquisitive travelers a fresh and unexpected insight into an entirely different aspect of Chicago's famous historic architecture.[176]

INTERLUDE: THE WOMEN'S WORLD'S FAIR

In 1917, Helen Bennett, a prominent Chicagoan and author of a book titled *Women and Work*, wrote, "Women have achieved more in the last ten years than in all the centuries preceding." But, she added, there was a problem: "Few people realize how much they have achieved."[177] Chicago women, being from the most inventive of cities, were the ones to fix this dilemma—by holding a world's fair for women. Bennett partnered with Ruth Hanna McCormick, another influential Chicagoan, and they began recruiting board members and fundraising.

When the Women's World's Fair opened on April 18, 1925, it occupied the entire main floor of the Chicago Furniture Mart. There were 280 booths showcasing over 100 occupations and professions in which women were active. There was a prospector, a plumber and "the lady who sells home-made candy."[178] Other women represented physicians, newspaper reporters, writers, advertising representatives, potters, inventors and so on. Among the artists were painters Mary Cassatt and Marie Laurencin and sculptor Malvina Hoffman.[179]

The fair was such a success that it was held annually for three more years, getting larger each time, and in 1927, it was moved to the Chicago Coliseum. By 1928, however, both Bennett and McCormick had gone on to other things, and Chicagoans had

Women's World's Fair souvenir program, 1925. *Courtesy of the Chicago History Museum, ICHi 037941.*

become preoccupied with planning a much larger fair—the Century of Progress Exposition of 1933. Nevertheless, the fair had proved its point: American women might have announced their liberation by shortening their skirts and drinking in speakeasies, but they also proclaimed it with a grand exposition, showing that no field of endeavor was off-limits.

6

JAZZ CAPITAL OF THE WORLD

In addition to all those nifty new kitchen appliances, Chicago bungalow dwellers had access to another exciting new gizmo: the phonograph.

Imagine a bunch of Chicago teenagers getting together in 1923. Kids couldn't go to nightclubs, but records were making it possible for them to hear jazz. These youngsters had gotten ahold of a stack of platters made by a hot new band called the New Orleans Rhythm Kings, who played at Chicago's Friar's Inn, a speakeasy on South Wabash Avenue. One of the youths, Jimmy McPartland, later recalled, "I'll tell you, we went out of our minds. Everybody flipped. It was wonderful….We stayed there from about three in the afternoon until eight at night, just listening to those records one after another, over and over again. Right then and there, we decided we would get a band and try to play like these guys."[180]

McPartland and his pals would go on to become known as the "Austin High Gang," a group of Chicagoans who would go on to have prominent jazz careers; besides cornetist McPartland, the band included saxophonist Bud Freeman and the clarinetist Frank Teschemaker. Other Chicago musicians who were inspired by or played with the Austin High Gang were Gene Krupa, Muggsy Spanier and Eddie Condon, all of whom became jazz stars. Meanwhile, Chicagoan Ben Pollack formed a band that, at one time or another, featured jazz giants Glenn Miller, Jack Teagarden, Harry James, Charlie Spivak and Chicago clarinetist Benny Goodman, who would go on to become the "King of Swing."

A NEW SOUND

In the 1920s, Chicago was "the jazz capital of the world."[181] The main reason for this was that most of the great New Orleans jazzmen who came north in the early twentieth century found the Windy City to be culturally receptive and financially rewarding. In 1918, the Black-owned newspaper the *Chicago Defender* asked: "Have you not heard that wonderful jazz music that the people of Chicago are going wild about? It's gripping the dancers of the Windy City….The jazz music is right at your door."[182] Jazz was party music and young people's music. In 1929, a *Chicago Tribune* columnist wrote that "an army of adolescents" had taken "complete charge of the music world."[183]

What was it like to experience jazz in 1920s Chicago? A vivid description of one of the more raucous clubs was given by the *Chicago Herald*, which offered this description of Schiller's Café on Thirty-First Street: "The shriek of women's drunken laughter rivaled the blatant scream of the imported New Orleans Jass [*sic*] Band, which never seemed to stop playing. Men and women sat, arms about each other, singing, shouting, making the night hideous, while their unfortunate brethren and sisters fought in vain to join them."[184] Around 1921, the Chicago reporter Ben Hecht reported on his visit to a jazz joint and recounted, "The cabaret floor, jammed, seems to be moving around like a groaning turnstile. Bodies are hidden. The spotlight from the balcony begins to throw a series of colors. Melody is lost. The jazz band is hammering like a mad blacksmith. *Whang! Bam! Whang! Bam!*" What especially struck Hecht was the "*umpah ump*" of the trombone, which set the band's relentless beat:

> *Umpah ump is the soul of things. Cadenzas, glissandos, arpeggios, chromatics, syncopations, blue melodies—these are the embroidery of sound. From year to year, these change, these pass. Only the umpah ump remains. And tonight, the trombone player plays what he will play a thousand nights from tonight—umpah ump. The bassoon and the bull fiddle—they umpah ump along….The feet dancing on the crowded cabaret floor listen cautiously for the trombone, the bassoon and the bull fiddle. They have a liaison with the umpah umps—the feet….Civilizations have risen, fallen and risen again. Armies, gods, races have been chewed into mist by the years. But the thumping remains.*[185]

Colored lights, thumping music, ecstatic youthful dancers—it sounds uncannily like a modern dance club.

New Orleans was the primary incubator of the new jazz music, and the musicians who brought jazz to Chicago were almost exclusively from the Crescent City; although the tale that the jazzmen came north after the military closed the red-light district known as Storyville in 1917 is a myth. For one thing, Storyville's dance halls and saloons remained open, and jazz was still played there. For another thing, jazz didn't emerge from bordellos. The early jazz bands had plenty of places to play—on riverboats, in parades, at picnics, in theaters, and at dances. As the jazz musician Sidney Bechet explained, "in those days, there was always some party going, some fish fry, and there was always some picnic around the lakes.…So, how can you say Jazz started in whorehouses when the musicianers didn't have no real need for them?…The way some people talk, you'd think we all sat and waited for Storyville to close."[186] Finally, jazz musicians began leaving New Orleans for Chicago long before 1917. Spencer Williams came to Chicago as early as 1907, and the pianist Tony (or "Toney") Jackson arrived around 1912. Jelly Roll Morton, the first true jazz composer, lived in Chicago from 1914 to 1917. The first White New Orleans jazz band to hit Chicago was Tom Brown's Dixieland Jass Band, which arrived in 1915.

A lot of the jazz action could be found on the "Stroll," a section of South State Street that was the home of Black entertainment. The strip contained dozens of cafés, cabarets and dance halls featuring the new jazz music. Chicago-based jazz guitarist Eddie Condon once said, "I don't think so much good jazz was ever concentrated in so small an area. Around midnight, you could hold an instrument in the middle of the street, and the air would play it. That was music."[187] The most famous club on the Stroll was the Dreamland, which, as early as June 1917, showcased its own "Original Jazz Band." The stars who performed there included King Oliver, Louis Armstrong, Sidney Bechet and Ethel Waters. The club also showcased Cook's Dreamland Ballroom Orchestra, which featured such New Orleans musicians as Freddie Keppard, Jimmie Noone, Andrew Hilaire and John St. Cyr. Another New Orleans jazzman who played in Chicago was Emanuel, or Manuel, Perez, a cornet player who arrived in 1915. Sidney Bechet himself made his first appearance in Chicago in 1917.

Downtown clubs also featured New Orleans musicians, but these performers were White. In January 1915, a banjo player named Bert Kelly and his band began appearing at the College Inn in the Hotel Sherman. The two most famous bands were the group led by trombonist Tom "Red" Brown and Stein's Dixieland Jass Band, which evolved into the Original Dixieland Jazz Band (ODJB), the first jazz band, Black or White, to make records. Another celebrated White jazz band was the New Orleans Rhythm Kings (NORK), led by cornet player Paul Mares. Louis Armstrong bought all their records and once wrote, "Oh what a band they had."[188] Among the wannabe musicians who heard the NORK during their engagement at the Friar's Inn was the teenaged Leon Bix Beiderbecke from Davenport, Iowa. Bix went on to become, after Armstrong, the premier cornet player of the Jazz Age, crafting a lyrical style that contrasted with Armstrong's flamboyance (see "Interlude: Jazz Me Blues"). It was at the Friar's Inn that Bix met a piano player from Indiana University named Hoagy Carmichael, who was soon to become one of America's best-known songwriters.

One reminiscence from Chicago blues pianist Art Hodes is a reminder that jazz was sometimes only a part of a wider array of entertainment presented in a café. "If it was a real class spot," he said, "it sported a five-piece band and an intermission piano player and singers. A floor show would consist of an emcee, a line of girls, the singers in the place—the band was strictly for background and a little dancing."[189] Nowadays, people usually go to one kind of place to eat (a restaurant) and another kind of place to dance (a club). Our imaginary visitor to Chicago in the Jazz Age would have found a great many places that offered both.

Some of the best-remembered trends of the Jazz Age came with the flood of new dances that were done to the accompaniment of jazz bands in nightclubs, dance halls, hotels and even schools, and Chicago, as the capital of jazz, was at the heart of this development. A writer for the show business newspaper *Variety* went so far as to say Chicago "started the metropolitan dancing craze."[190] These new dances were described as "sensual, sexual, and energetic."[191] Several were "animal" dances, such as the cat step, turkey trot, grizzly bear, camel walk and bunny hug. The most popular was probably the Charleston; others included the varsity drag, the shimmy, the black bottom, and the Lindy hop.[192] In 1922, the authorities closed the Entertainers Café on the South Side for being "indecent and immoral." Two performers, Julia Rector and Bertha Ricks, were arrested for doing the shimmy, a dance in which the shoulders were rapidly moved back and forth. At a court hearing on January 17, Rector testified that the shimmy was not at all indecent—"not as I dance it." About a week later, the judge found Rector guilty of "improper performance" and fined her $200. His verdict blasted jazz dancing in general: "This case smacks of the barbarism of the jungle. The very music was obscene....That these things happen...in a so-called civilized community, where decency and religion are presumed to be supreme, must cause the average Chicagoan to hang

THE SONG THAT DEFINED A CITY
After Chicago bandleaders Paul
Biese and Frank Westphal wrote (with
Jimmy Steiger) this catchy number,
Chicago became known as "that
toddlin' town." *Author's collection.*

his head in shame."[193] The shimmy probably began in Black nightclubs, but the two performers who are most identified with it were White women with Chicago connections. Beatrice "Bee" Palmer, who was born in the Windy City in 1894, began performing in Chicago nightclubs before World War I. After relocating to New York, she appeared in the *Midnight Frolic of 1918* and began calling herself the "shimmy queen." Gilda Gray, who was born Marianna Michalska in Poland in 1901, grew up in Wisconsin and came to Chicago around 1918. Soon, the beautiful Gray was also a Ziegfeld star, appearing in the *Ziegfeld Follies* on Broadway, where her success was instrumental in furthering the shimmy mania.

For Chicagoans, probably the most significant new jazz number was the song that begins "Chicago, Chicago, that toddlin' town / Chicago, Chicago, I'll show you around." A century after it was written in 1922, people still sing Fred Fisher's "Chicago." But what does *toddlin'* mean? People might picture someone lurching down the street from too much bootleg gin—stumbling, that is, like a toddler. But *toddlin'* has a specific meaning. The toddle was one of the many new jazz dances. In late 1916, the *New York Times* published an article titled "We Must Toddle in 1917." It reported that the Inner Circle, a group "devoted to the development of the modern dance," had chosen the toddle as the fad of 1917. Soon after, the Chicago newspaper the *Day Book*

HEARD COAST TO COAST
Because their radio broadcasts spanned the nation, Chicago's most famous jazz ensemble was the Coon-Sanders Original Nighthawk Orchestra. They played at Don Roth's celebrated Blackhawk Restaurant throughout the 1920s. Their hit song "Angry" (1925) remained popular through the 1950s. *Author's collection.*

FROM JAZZ TO SWING
The hugely popular ensemble headed by songwriter Isham Jones ("I'll See You in My Dreams" and "It Had to Be You") exemplified the evolution of the small jazz band into the larger swing orchestra. The Rainbo Gardens and the College Inn were just two of the clubs they played in Chicago. *Author's collection.*

ran an article titled "Can You Toddle?—Better Learn—It's All the Rage."[194] In 1921, two Chicago bandleaders, Paul Biese and Frank Westphal, along with songwriter Jimmy Steiger, published a tune simply called "Toddle." This song was recorded at least twice and had a national following.

In 1921, the *Chicago Tribune* sent out a reporter known only as "Martha" to survey the "why and what of modern dancing." She started at a South Side black-and-tan (a club in which the races mingled) called the Lorraine Gardens. The dance floor was crowded, which was the situation in most clubs. Jazzman Warren "Baby" Dodds, for example, once recalled that "the people came to dance....The music was so wonderful that they had to do something, even if there was only room to bounce around."[195] Martha reported that couples were "unanimously Caucasian" but then contradicted herself. "I turn quickly," she wrote, "to see a white woman—clad tastefully in black, red-trimmed hat and dress—pass my table in the embrace of a tall, ebon Negro."[196] Martha then moved to a "honka-tonk" on Clark and Erie Streets, where she found the dancing to be "naughty and hideous." "It is the black belt Babylon over again," she commented, "except all the revelers are white."[197] Next, Martha took herself to a high-class cabaret—the Ansonia at Broadway and Wilson Street. There, she wrote, "the citizens of uptown Chicago remain true to their station; their dance is a cross between that of the honka-tonk and that of the high-born children of wealth." Finally, she went into the Green Mill: "In the semi-twilight of a room which teems with barbarous, pulsing jazz music, the occupants of many score tables are going through the slow, methodical shaking which they call dancing."

As early as September 1921, Martha was pronouncing the toddle "as dead as the notorious door nail." It was being replaced by something called the "Mexatang."[198] And yet, in that very same month, the proprietors of Chicago's Midway Gardens, the South Side entertainment emporium designed by Frank Lloyd Wright, announced a remodeling that would give the structure "the largest toddle floor in the world."[199] Restaurants were beginning to create what were called "action environments"—areas cleared of tables in which patrons could dance or entertainers could perform. Formerly, entertainment was presented on a stage that was raised above the audience, but with action environments, everything was on one level, creating a greater sense of informality. Restaurant owners welcomed audience participation; some provided noisemakers, while others encouraged diners to "make their own jazz" by banging their silverware on the tables. Performers liked the new closeness because it was easier to collect tips.[200]

Our imaginary visitor would surely have wanted to hear the Chicago bands that, because of radio and widely distributed recordings, had national reputations. Although New York remained the musical theater and publishing center, record companies sent representatives to scout out and record Chicago's celebrated bands, who were considered the most progressive in the nation. At the Blackhawk Restaurant was the renowned Coon-Sanders Orchestra, a ten-member ensemble founded by drummer Carlton Coon and pianist Joe Sanders in Kansas City in 1919. As early as 1922, the band began broadcasting, and their fan base grew to be immense. It was big news when they relocated to Chicago in 1924, and it was even bigger news when they began broadcasting on WGN, Chicago's leading radio station, two years later.

Isham Jones, who played at both the College Inn and the Rainbo Gardens, was one of the central figures in creating what became known as the "big band" sound that dominated the Swing Era. He developed a "style that stressed a 'singing' delivery of long, smoothly melodic lines" and an "ensemble sound rich in mid-range sonorities."[201] In 1920, Jones and his Rainbo Orchestra traveled to New York and cut thirty-seven sides for

CLAIM TO FAME
After appearing on Broadway, Beatrice "Bee" Palmer, who was born in Chicago in 1894, began calling herself the "shimmy queen." *Author's collection.*

Brunswick Records. Although some characteristics of the band's sound, such as the inclusion of a violin and the absence of a trumpet, were a bit old-fashioned, Jones's extensive work on the saxophone, an instrument that was fairly new to pop music, gave it a progressive tinge. After these recordings, Jones went on to have success as a songwriter, writing the standards "I'll See You in My Dreams," "The One I Love (Belongs to Somebody Else)" and "It Had to Be You."[202] In 1928, the *Chicagoan* praised Jones's band for avoiding the "dance tripe" played by other bands and playing "the music from *Show-Boat*, the *Connecticut Yankee*, and *Present Arms*," which were contemporary Broadway musicals with scores by distinguished composers.[203]

Among other Chicago ensembles that left a legacy of recordings was the Benson Orchestra of Chicago, which recorded more than one hundred sides for RCA Victor between 1920 and 1926. Edgar Benson himself was not the group's leader, but he was the most powerful impresario in Chicago; a 1922 advertisement stated that he controlled "five symphony orchestras, nine brass bands, thirty dance orchestras, six jazz bands, [and] ten novelty orchestras."[204] Under conductor Roy Bargy, the band generally recorded two kinds of songs—the fox trot and the faster one-step, which provided

SHIMMY AND SHAKE
A major Chicago-based shimmy star was the glamorous Gilda Gray, born Marianna Michalska in Poland in 1901. *From Wikimedia Commons.*

the "jazzier" of the sides. On April 11, 1921, the group recorded a polished rendition of the "Toddle."

Tenor saxophonist Paul Biese played in many Chicago venues, including the Marigold Gardens, the Bismarck Hotel and the Edgewater Beach Hotel. After besting seventeen other dance bands in a contest, Biese advertised his group as "Paul Biese and His Champion Band." It's an intriguing bit of historical trivia to note that Biese, whose weight once ballooned to nearly four hundred pounds, was in the Chicago papers in 1920 for having had fifty pounds of fat surgically removed from his waist, one of the earliest recorded examples of liposuction. His doctor, Max Thorek, explained, "It's not a dangerous operation, but it is one that has not been performed many times."[205] The procedure didn't do much for Biese's long-term health; he died in 1925 at the age of thirty-eight. Between 1922 and 1924, bandleader Paul Westphal, one of the composers of "Toddle," made a series of records in Chicago for Columbia Records. Historians credit the recordings for their ingenious arrangements and Westphal's keen appropriation of the best sounds of other contemporary groups, both White and Black.

Finally, during the early years of the Jazz Age, Chicago's Paul Ash was "probably the highest-paid bandleader in the United States."[206] His ensemble didn't play nightclubs or restaurants but theaters; in the 1920s, many movie palaces began featuring dance bands. In May 1925, Ash, who had movie star looks and was called the "Rajah of Jazz," began a stint at the McVickers Theater, where he was a sensation. Ash didn't just wave a baton but danced, jumped and wiggled his rear end. After Ash, bandleaders didn't have to exactly leave their feet, but they had to project some personality. The music that Ash recorded is enjoyable, but it's more "jazz-inflected" than hardcore jazz. In the mid-1920s, pop music began to separate into two genres: "sweet" and "hot," and Ash's music was sweet. With the rise of sweet music, the association of dance bands with low dives and speakeasies transformed into something with more middle-class respectability. While the more elegant dance bands performed sweet music in ballrooms and theaters, the earlier, rougher Dixieland/New Orleans style remained but was largely found in clubs and cabarets.

Many contemporary observers thought jazz was downright dangerous, and self-appointed guardians of morality viewed the era as one of decadence—the manners were dreadful, the clothes were scandalous and Prohibition, which once promised to purify American morality, seemed to be corrupting it even more. At a board meeting of the General Federation of Women's Clubs in Chicago, one infuriated member said, "Jazz music is a form of immorality....It is music gone wild, and...it throws the human system out of joint....It not only injures the morals of those who come under its influence, but it is un-American."[207] When, in 1922, Judge Arnold Heap of the morals court fined a dancer for performing the shimmy, he delivered a rebuke that said, in part, "If such entertainments are tolerated, it means the debauching of society, the corruption of the community, and the destruction of the moral stamina of the nation."[208] In 1926, a New York physician named Harry Gilbert warned that the Charleston could lead to, among other things, "heart trouble, nervous diseases, fallen arches, broken ankles, strained backs and fallen abdominal organs."[209] But the Charleston and other "stomping" dances were not the worst of it. The slower, sensuous dances, of which the toddle was one (so was the shimmy), were the dances that were truly shocking, as they promoted physical contact (the "Toddle" sheet music depicts a sleek couple clenched in an embrace while dancing). It's no wonder Chicago's superintendent of schools prohibited the toddle at school dances.[210] Various organizations, including the National Association of Ball Room Proprietors and Managers, gave exhibitions on the proper decorum that was to be observed while dancing, and "experts" gave professional opinions on the harmful effect of the new steps. An organization called the Juvenile Protective Association sent "chaperones" to dance halls to monitor the situation. If a chaperone spied a clutching couple dancing with little foot movement, he would call out, "Get off that dime, man. Let's move it around."[211]

Jazz, in effect, was providing the soundtrack for what was America's first sexual revolution. As historians John D'Emilio and Estelle B. Freedman have explained, "Among the many changes during this period, two stand out as emblematic of this new sexual order: the redefinition of womanhood to include eroticism, and the decline of public reticence about sex. By 1920, the separate spheres, so critical in the construction of nineteenth-century middle-class sexual mores, had collapsed."[212] A contemporary writer named Elmer T. Clark wrote that the world was "threatened with having its confidence in and respect for women undermined….Their familiar association with the men, their profligate use of cigarettes…the masculinity which comes from doing the work of men, the increasing carelessness in the matter of personal appearance….Then in connection with this there is the awful deluge of vice which has degraded so many thousands."[213] As historian Simon Baatz has put it, "many White Protestant Americans" found the Jazz Age "deeply troubling"; "the traditional morality, centered on work, discipline, and self-denial, had evaporated, and in its place, there was a culture of self-indulgence. There were no longer any social restraints; each individual now sought self-fulfillment and self-realization in an unceasing pursuit of pleasure."[214]

For Americans, in general—but for Chicagoans, especially—exhibit A in the corruption of American youth by jazz and other modern depravities was the famous murder trial of Leopold and Loeb. Nathan F. Leopold Jr. and Richard A. Loeb were two wealthy Chicago youths who were so brilliant that they graduated from college while they were still in their teens. To prove their

JAZZ-MAD KILLERS
The trial of Richard Loeb (*left*) and Nathan Leopold (*right*) for the wanton killing of a fourteen-year-old boy was called the "trial of the century" and remains one of the most famous trials in Chicago history. Many commentators blamed their warped worldview on the corrupting influence of modern culture, especially jazz. *From Wikimedia Commons.*

brainpower and claim status as one of the supermen, or "Übermenschen," prophesied by the voguish German philosopher Friedrich Nietzsche, they decided to commit the "perfect crime." They kidnaped and killed fourteen-year-old Bobby Franks and left his body in a marshland near the Indiana state line. Police easily solved their "perfect crime," and the resulting trial dominated the national headlines for weeks. The killers' families retained the nation's most famous lawyer, Clarence Darrow of Chicago, who managed to save them from the gallows and had them sentenced to life in prison. Pundits spilled oceans of ink in explaining the decadent spirit behind the murder. A writer for the *Chicago Tribune* surmised that Leopold and Loeb "were jaded by the jazz life of gin and girls so that they needed as terrible a thing as murder to give them new thrills."[215] Similarly, Max P. Schlapp, a neurology professor in New York, warned that America was entering a period of "emotional instability" that was causing "crime, feeble-mindedness, insanity." This instability was said to be the product of automobiles, movies and "the phenomenal sweep of jazz across the country."[216] Judge Ben Lindsey of Denver, considered an authority on juvenile delinquency, wrote that the killing was "a new kind of murder with a new kind of cause. That cause is to be found in the modern mentality and modern freedom of youth....Do you not, then, see this is more than the story of murder? It is the story of modern youth, the story of modern parents, the story of modern education....The indifference to the rights of others in stealing of automobiles, in joy rides, jazz parties, petting parties, freedom in sex relations and the mania for speed at every turn."[217] Newspaper columnist Winifred Black summed it up: the murder of Bobby Franks, she wrote, was the "fruit of the Jazz Age."

America's Greatest Musician

Jelly Roll Morton, Sidney Bechet, Freddie Keppard, Bert Kelly, the Original Dixieland Jazz Band, the New Orleans Rhythm Kings, Isham Jones, Coon and Sanders and Bix Beiderbecke all played their part in making Chicago a jazz capital, but the city's most significant moment in jazz came when King Oliver, the leading jazzman in New Orleans, arrived in the Windy City in 1918. The great cornetist played in different clubs until June 1922, when he took up residence at the Royal Gardens, soon renamed the Lincoln Gardens. The *Chicago Defender* reported that Oliver's ensemble was the "razziest, jazziest band you ever heard" and "the finest Negro jazz band that ever came out of New Orleans."[218]

As good as Oliver's group was, it became even better when Oliver summoned from New Orleans the twenty-one-year-old Louis Armstrong. Armstrong was born on August 4, 1901, in a section of New Orleans that was so tough, it was known as "the Battlefield." His father abandoned the family when Louis was an infant, and Louis dropped out of school in the fifth grade. The neighborhood kids doled out nicknames for their peers, and the one that stuck for Louis was Satchmo, short for "satchelmouth" (in his later years, his friends more often called him Pops). Around the age of ten, Louis was arrested for firing a pistol into the air on New Year's Eve. He was sent to the Colored Waifs' Home, where he joined the band, and his uncanny talent was recognized. After his release, he began hanging out with older musicians; King Oliver became both his teacher and something of a substitute father. When Armstrong played on Mississippi riverboats, he learned how to read music, and by the time Oliver called him to Chicago, Armstrong was a skilled professional. Armstrong quickly proved himself equal and then superior to his mentor, with whom he stayed until 1924. Armstrong would go on to become not only America's greatest jazz musician but also, arguably, America's greatest musician—period.

In later life, Armstrong lived in New York City, but it was in Chicago that he modernized American popular music. Between 1925 to 1928, he organized the bands the Hot Fives and the Hot Sevens, which recorded some sixty sides for Okeh records. If, as the jazz writer Gary Giddens has said, Armstrong is America's Bach, then the recordings he made with the Hot Fives and the Hot Sevens are his *St. Matthew Passion.* (Comparisons of Armstrong's work to classical music are not uncommon.[219]) A vital aspect of the Hot Fives, and Hot Sevens' records is that they were made for listening, not dancing—a major step in the development of jazz as art.

In "Struttin' with Some Barbecue," which Armstrong recorded in Chicago with the Hot Fives on December 9, 1927, we find one of the first instances of Armstrong refining the jazz solo by transforming the concept of improvisation. We know now that some of his most celebrated solos were not improvisations but compositions that were worked out in advance, making Armstrong a composer in the true sense of the word. Like his crafting of solos, his melodies would also prove his prowess as a composer. Several of the recordings, such as "Potato Head Blues," "Muskrat Ramble," "Ory's Creole Trombone" and "Basin Street Blues," were New Orleans standards, but others, such as "Struttin' with Some Barbecue," "Heebie Jeebies," "Yes I'm in the Barrel," "Skid-Dat-De-Dat," "That's When I'll Come Back to You" and "Hotter Than That," were

AMERICA'S BACH
During the years he lived in Chicago, Louis Armstrong not only became America's greatest jazz musician, but he also became, arguably, America's greatest musician of any kind. *Courtesy of the Library of Congress.*

composed by Louis himself, with help from Lil Hardin Armstrong, his wife at the time and the piano player in the group. As he later recalled, "It's a funny thing how I used to sit on the back steps of Lil's home and write five and six songs a day....Just lead sheets....And Lil would put the other parts in them...cornet, clarinet, trombone, et cetera."[220]

At the same time, Armstrong was perfecting the idea of "swing," playing behind or ahead of the beat to give the music an infectious lilt—a concept that dominated American popular music for a long time (the 1930s and 1940s became known as the "Swing Era"). The Hot Fives, and Hot Sevens' records also featured Armstrong as a vocalist, and his loose, jazz-inflected style influenced almost every singer who came after him and fixed the style of pop singing for decades. "Heebie Jeebies," which he recorded in February 1926, was, for many people, their introduction to "scat" singing, or vocalizing without words to imitate an instrument. Armstrong's extensive use of the recording studio in the 1920s prefigured how he would later utilize technology (recordings, radio, movies, television) to reach first a national and then global audience. Armstrong and other Chicago jazz musicians were most likely the first to appreciate the importance of recordings as a means of finding fame (and employment).[221] More than one music critic has drawn a direct line from Armstrong to rock, soul and hip hop. Musician/writer Will Layman once wrote, "His feeling for the individual expression of time didn't just set up Basie and Bird, Miles and Marsalis. Without Armstrong, there's no James Brown or Johnny Cash, there's no Sinatra and no Kanye."[222]

Thomas Brothers, one of Armstrong's most recent biographers, summed up Armstrong's art: "He was not only a great trumpeter but also a great singer and entertainer; further, he was a great melodist, who invented a melodic idiom of jazz solo playing that became tremendously influential. That's a lot of greatness in one person." Brothers added, "It all fell into place in the decade or so after 1922, which was also the period that found him at his peak."[223] The process occurred in Chicago, and it's hard to imagine that any other city could have provided the environment needed for Armstrong to flourish.

INTERLUDE: JAZZ ME BLUES

In the Jazz Age, hearing jazz wasn't enough for many youngsters. They also wanted to play it. So, they bought instruments and formed little groups—the 1920s version of the garage rock band. Few of these ensembles went anywhere, but one that did was a Midwestern troupe called the Wolverines.

The Wolverines' first record was "Jazz Me Blues." The story goes that when the pioneering New Orleans jazz cornetist Emmett Hardy (1903–1925) first heard it, he said, "I know who that is. That's a kid from Davenport by the name of Leon Beiderbecke."[224] Even then the sound was unmistakable.

Leon "Bix" Beiderbecke was a musical prodigy, and when he first heard jazz records at the age of fifteen, he discovered his mission. He taught himself how to play the cornet and soaked up the new sound in Chicago, listening to White bands at the Friar's Inn and Black bands on the South Side. He joined the Wolverines in 1923 at the age of twenty and recorded "Jazz Me Blues" in February 1924. It was, say Bix's biographers, "a pioneer

The Wolverine Orchestra. Bix Beiderbecke is seated in the center with his cornet. *From Wikimedia Commons.*

record, introducing a musician of great originality."[225] It was a new sound: lyrical and singing, not explosive and sizzling like Louis Armstrong but contemplative. It made Bix a star—one that burned fiercely until his death from alcoholism and pneumonia at the age of twenty-eight.

Bix's death was so early and tragic that he became a kind of jazz martyr. Jazz critic Benny Green labeled him "jazz's number one saint," and jazz historian Gunther Schuller said that just as F. Scott Fitzgerald became the symbol of Jazz Age literature, so Bix became the symbol of Jazz Age music.[226]

7

"GUGGLE AND GLUB"

The Chicago Art Scene

Having visited Art Deco architecture and design, moderne electrical appliances and transformational musical innovations, we move on to some other manifestations of Chicago's innovative cultural life during the Jazz Age.

The Dil Pickle Club

Down in the alley, hard by the park,
In a helix nook that is grim and dark,
Where the intellectuals gather to guggle and glub,
You know what I mean—the Dil Pickle Club!
—Eddie Guilbert

Chicago's Dil Pickle Club (the fact that the owner spelled "dill" with one "l" is a sign that unconventionality was the theme of the place) was, according to historian Franklin Rosemont, "far and away the best-loved, most notorious, most stimulating, and most influential little gathering place in the city's history."

In the early years of the Jazz Age, Chicago's neighborhoods were not vast, and diverse city zones coexisted cheek to cheek. For example, as mentioned earlier, just south of the Gold Coast was Tower Town, which was, to use the word that was then in vogue, *bohemian*. The residents tended to be artistic, unconventional, educated and short of funds—what we now call "alternative." Interestingly, one observer in the 1920s observed that Tower Town was "predominantly a women's bohemia": "It is the young women who open most of the studios, run most of the tearooms and restaurants, most of the little art shops and bookstalls, manage the exhibits and little theaters."[227]

Tower Town was the perfect location for the Dil Pickle Club. Although it wasn't owned by women, they made up a prominent portion of its clientele. The founder was Ontario-born John Archibald "Jack" Jones, who had a long history of involvement in leftist/labor causes, most notably the Industrial Workers of the World (IWW), also known as the "Wobblies," a fierce anti-capitalist group founded in Chicago that terrified early twentieth-century conservatives. Jones founded the Dil Pickle Club around 1914 (historians have found it difficult to determine the exact year of its founding).

The club was first located, as Jones once described it, "on the dry end of Pearson Street (the other end runs into Lake Michigan)."[228] When the landlord raised the rent, Jones relocated a short distance away to 18 Tooker Alley in the heart of Tower Town. Nearby was a park that was officially named Washington Square Park, but it was unofficially called Bughouse Square. It was dedicated to free speech—anyone could get up on a soapbox and hold forth on just about any topic. The speakers were jokingly known as "ozone orators," and on fair-weather weekends as many as ten thousand people would crowd on the green to hear two or three dozen of them. Popular topics were the labor movement, atheism and other religious subjects and the theories of Freud and Marx. One contemporary observer said, "All their arguments come down to one or the other of two propositions: the economic system is all wrong, or there is no God."[229] Frank O. Beck, who knew the square well, left a few descriptions of its characters. The declaimers, he wrote, included "Christians, pagans, vegetarians, socialists, agnostics, atheists, single-taxers, communists and a full score of other rebels against the existing order, each the incarnation of some society-saving panacea." One of them, known as Wee Willie Winkle, would say, "If you guys had the brains to listen, I would teach you something," while Harry Batters, the "childhood buddy of Lenin," bragged that he lived for forty days on nothing but peanuts. Two women orators were Martha Begler and Kathleen Caldwell, whose message was "only fools think they are awake."[230] Bughouse Square has been called "not only the best-known free-speech center in Chicago, but also…the best-known outdoor place for radical oratory in the nation." The Dil Pickle Club was often called "the indoor Bughouse Square."[231] Close by was the

Radical Bookshop, which was owned and operated by Lillian Udell, a blind poet who, with her two daughters, would stage modern plays at the back of the store.

By the 1920s, the authors who had constituted the heroic age of Chicago literature, including Henry Blake Fuller, George Ade, Finley Peter Dunne, Frank Norris, Theodore Dreiser, Carl Sandburg, Hamlin Garland, Upton Sinclair, Edna Ferber, Edgar Lee Masters, Sherwood Anderson and Ben Hecht, had either declined or moved away (mostly to New York City). Hecht, who decamped for Hollywood, came to regret it: "We were all fools to have left Chicago. It was a town to play in, a town where you could stay yourself and where the hoots of the critics couldn't frighten your style or drain your soul."[232] The most prominent literary figure to come out of Chicagoland—Ernest Hemingway of Oak Park—made his fame and fortune in Paris and elsewhere.

Harriet Monroe was one of the few nationally known literary luminaries who chose to remain in the Windy City. In 1912, she founded the pathbreaking magazine *Poetry*, which historians of literature point to as one of the key drivers of modernism in the United States. Poets whose works appeared in *Poetry* included William Carlos Williams, T.S. Eliot and Wallace Stevens. Readers first encountered Carl Sandburg's "Chicago" ("Hog Butcher for the World...City of the Big Shoulders") in the magazine's March 1914 issue. Aside from Monroe, other Chicagoans who kept literary life alive were the aforementioned Lillian Udell, who operated the Radical Bookshop, and Fanny Butcher, a literary critic of the *Chicago Tribune* for forty years, who ran a bookstore across the street from the Art Institute from 1919 to 1927. She was friends with, among others, Carl Sandburg, Gertrude Stein, Willa Cather, H.L. Mencken, T.S. Eliot and Sinclair Lewis. Hemingway called her "the most loyal friend" he ever had.[233] Then there was Thomas Woods Stevens, first director of the Goodman Theatre, which opened in 1927.

Although Jack Jones was the proprietor of the Dil Pickle, the club's best-known figure was Dr. Ben Reitman, a kid from the roughest streets in Chicago who, with the help of a benevolent mentor, graduated from the American College of Medicine and Surgery in Chicago in 1904. He opened his office in a rough neighborhood, and, according to his biographer, "Underworld types and down-and-outs gravitated to Ben's office, as did prostitutes, pimps, dope addicts, and sexual perverts, all of whom began to call him 'Doc.'"[234] Reitman became the lover of Emma Goldman, the renowned anarchist, freethinker and feminist; together, they got into trouble for illegally distributing literature on birth control. In 1908, Reitman founded what he called the

Hobo College. At this charitable institution, which lasted for nearly thirty years and changed locations almost yearly, homeless men and "Skid Row" residents could hear lectures, forge friendships, receive medical care and find help securing a job. They could also cadge a few bucks from Dr. Reitman (the college once briefly offered a course on panhandling). In 1917, the Chicago Health Department hired Reitman to attend to the city's homeless. At the Dil Pickle Club, Doc Reitman gave such lectures as "Satisfying Sex Needs Without Trouble" and "Favorite Methods of Suicide." He had a knack for getting the club's doings into the newspapers. As Reitman put it, "When I came on the scene, the Dil Pickle Club was still an unknown club." He said, "I became chairman and press agent, and in six months, it was one of the most popular and well known forums in the city."[235]

The Dil Pickle was in what has been described as an old barn, although, over time, Jones purchased and adapted some adjacent structures. Written on the low, orange entrance door were the words "Step High. Stoop Low. Leave Your Dignity Outside." In 1931, reporter John Drury wrote: "The walls are adorned with garish paintings; the dance room is dark and dusty and dimly-lit; the little theater is awfully little; the garden is popular on summer nights; and the coffee shop serves coffee and a few light foods that are tolerable."[236] Alcohol was not served, but during Prohibition, Jones sold quarts of ginger ale for $1.50 (presumably a fair price for customers bearing hip flasks). It was in the café room that customers engaged in intense conversations and arguments. Burton Rascoe, writing in the *New York Tribune*, remarked that the club was "equally attended by North Shore society leaders, pickpockets, morons, soapbox theists, University of Chicago professors, and derelicts of all kinds."[237]

The chatter in the café was often about what the customers had heard in the adjacent room, which was a combination lecture hall and dance space that held about seven hundred people. There, the famous—and sometimes infamous—Dil Pickle lectures were given. The topics illustrate how what we think of as a modern outlook began taking form in the Jazz Age. For example, birth control was nearly taboo in public discussion, but listeners in the lecture hall heard plenty about it, most notably from Ettie Rout, a venereal disease specialist who had written a notorious "safe sex" manual titled *Safe Marriage: A Return to Sanity*. Same-sex attraction was, in the same manner, discussed at the Dil Pickle when it was not mentioned in polite conversation elsewhere. In 1920, Jack Ryan presented a lecture on "The Third Sex," and eleven years later, the German physician Magnus Hirschfeld presented a talk called "In Defense of Homosexuality." In

Tower Town, it was possible to live as an openly gay person with nearly complete freedom. One observer reported, "A number of times, I have followed a cab…the lights of my car revealing its occupants, two men or two girls, fondling each other." He recounted a roving batch of men known as the "blue birds" who would cruise for partners along the lakefront.[238] It was in Chicago in 1924 that Henry Gerber founded the Society for Human Rights, the first gay rights organization in the United States; his home in Old Town is now an LGBTQ landmark. In this matter, Chicago was the leader of a trend. "The early decades of the twentieth century," wrote historian Joshua Zeitz, "saw the emergence of subterranean gay subcultures" in quite a few American cities.[239]

Although most clubs and restaurants north of the Loop did not admit Black patrons, there was no color line at the Dil Pickle. Black luminaries who appeared there included choreographer Katherine Dunham; poet and novelist Jean Toomer; dancer Garrison Williams, who was famous for his "Walk the Dog"; and former prizefighter Jack Johnson, who had found a second career as the leader of a jazz band. Many jazz ensembles played at the Dil Pickle, and playwright William Moore gave a lecture there titled "Jazz, the Hope of the Nation."[240] Even interracial romances blossomed at the club; Edna Fine Dexter recalled "a brilliant Negro whose first name was Claude," who "would entrance us with his pyrotechnics in mathematics and logic. He was a wistful boy and went around with a Russian girl named Anna."[241]

The club's other lecturers were impressively intellectual. Henri Peyre of Yale, for example, talked about modern French literature—his presentation seems to have introduced surrealism to America—and A.C. Lunn of the University of Chicago explained Einstein's theory of relativity. The club's other speakers included attorney Clarence Darrow, Ben Hecht, socialist Eugene V. Debs, novelist Sherwood Anderson and poets Carl Sandburg, William Carlos Williams, Vachel Lindsay and Djuna Barnes. In the hayloft was a room for artists—"often a party of visitors stood by, waiting to be shocked by the nude subject."[242] And finally, the Pickle Players made an important contribution to the little theater movement. The works of Ibsen and Shaw were staged, as were dramas by local playwrights (Hecht had a couple of works presented there). A reporter named Red Terry insisted that the Dil Pickle Club was "the intellectual center of America." When asked why New York's Greenwich Village didn't deserve the title, he explained that although the village might be the "artistic" center, it was only at the Dil Pickle that one could find "the bums who talked like professors."[243]

By the 1930s, the Dil Pickle's fortunes had waned. One account says that gangsters infiltrated the place and demanded a cut. Meanwhile, several regulars opened clubs of their own. Finally, the nearby New England Congregational Church pressured the police to do something; the authorities unearthed an old statute that said a dance hall was not permitted within one hundred feet of a church, and the club was shuttered in 1933. Jack Jones died seven years later.

Archibald Motley: Painter of the Jazz Age

Historians of art in the United States generally divide the period between World War I and World War II into two camps—one that followed the radical cubist/abstractionist innovations from Europe and another that employed a stylized realism inspired by American subject matter. The latter group includes Thomas Hart Benton, Charles Burchfield, John Steuart Curry, Edward Hopper, Georgia O'Keeffe and Grant Wood, whose iconic *American Gothic* was first exhibited at the Art Institute of Chicago in 1930. Other Chicago artists were active during the Jazz Age but are not as famous as these; they include Raymond Jonson, Beatrice Levy, Frances Foy, Anthony Angarola, Emil Armin and Louis Grell, who, when he was a teacher at the Art Institute, had a student named Walt Disney. In 1921, a few avant-garde Chicago artists formed a short-lived society called Cor Ardens, or "Ardent Hearts," that mounted a show in November 1922. One notable Chicago abstract artist was Paul Kelpe; another was William Schwartz, who produced a series of sixty-six abstract works that he called "symphonic forms." A Chicago painter of greater fame was Ivan Albright, whose unsettling portraits of people in varying states of deterioration made him the perfect choice to paint the ghastly portrait used in the macabre *Picture of Dorian Gray* film (1945).[244] One Chicago artist of the period, however, is much better known than all the others.

Archibald J. Motley Jr. was, as the art historian Richard J. Powell put it, "the quintessential jazz painter, without equal."[245] Because he was most active in the 1920s and 1930s, Motley is often associated with the Harlem Renaissance, that flowering of Black literature, culture and art that took place in New York City and included such luminaries as Langston Hughes, Zora Neale Hurston, Countee Cullen and W.E.B. Du Bois. Motley's painting *Blues* (1929), for example, is on the cover of both *The Cambridge Companion to the Harlem Renaissance* and *Rhapsodies in Black: Art of the Harlem Renaissance*.[246]

But Motley was a pure Chicagoan, with little connection either to New York or the Harlem Renaissance. Although he knew some of the leaders of the Harlem Renaissance, he was mostly unimpressed by New York's Black artists. He even once said that when it came to painting, "There was no Renaissance."[247] But about the Windy City, Motley said, "I can't find any place like Chicago. You know, I love this place."[248] As the art historian Wendy Greenhouse has put it:

> *With few exceptions, Motley pursued his goal single-mindedly, choosing as his perennial subject the Black community of his hometown, Chicago, where he lived for virtually his entire career. In portraits and genre scenes, he surveyed the rich variety of life in the area of Chicago known as the Black Belt, from its elegant night spots to the private interiors of its middle class to the lively social kaleidoscope of its street life.[249]*

Motley was born in the same city as Louis Armstrong—New Orleans—on October 7, 1891. His family moved to Chicago when he was a toddler. The Motleys settled in the Englewood neighborhood, which was then mostly White, and young Archibald went to nearly all-White elementary schools. His mother was a schoolteacher, and his father, a respected Pullman porter, was one of the founders of the Brotherhood of Sleeping Car Porters, one of the first Black labor unions.[250] The Motleys were Roman Catholic and worshipped at St. Brendan's Church. Archibald was fond of sketching in the margins of his school textbooks, and tolerant teachers recognized his obvious talent for drawing. As he got older, Motley discovered the diversions of the nearby Black Bronzeville neighborhood, including the Stroll. As early as fifth grade, he once recalled, he made sketches at a Black-owned pool hall. His daughter-in-law Valerie Browne once said, "He was kind of an insider-outsider. He came from a middle-class Black family in Englewood, a neighborhood that was more White than Black. He would go to Bronzeville because he was so taken with it and the people there. He was almost like an anthropologist."[251]

Motley's depictions of Black life are observant and affectionate but sometimes border on sarcasm—although Motley saw his approach as objective and candid. As he put it, "with the progress the Negro has made, he is deserving to be represented in his true perspective, with dignity, honesty, integrity, intelligence, and understanding.…The Negro is no more the lazy, happy-go-lucky, shiftless person he was shortly after the Civil War. Progress has changed all this. In my paintings, I have tried to paint the Negro as I have seen him and as I feel him in myself without adding or detracting, just being frankly honest."[252] Motley came from the Black elite, and his Creole and Catholic background set him apart from most of his peers. His family was numbered among Black Chicago's old settlers—those who arrived before the Great Migration—and many of the old settlers had reservations about the newcomers. One of them went so far as to comment that the Black individuals who were in Chicago before the war "were just about civilized and didn't make apes out of themselves like the ones who came here during 1918."[253] Motley's pride in his background helps explain what art historian Phoebe Wolfskill has said—that Motley's genre paintings fall "somewhere between redemption and satire."[254] As Motley himself explained, "To me, it seems that pictures portraying the suffering, sorrow, and, at times, the childlike abandon of the Negro; the dance, the song, the hilarious moments when a bit of Jazz predominates, would do much to bring about better relations, a better understanding between the races, white and colored."[255]

Motley's interest in art continued at Englewood High School, where he learned drawing, lettering, chalk and charcoal sketching and the art of perspective. By chance, a passenger on one of Motley's father's trains was Frank Gunsaulus, the president of Chicago's Armour Institute, who, after meeting a young Archibald, agreed to fund his first year at the School of the Art Institute of Chicago, which was one of the first American art academies to admit Black art students.[256] Motley's training in all aspects of painting and drawing was solid; he showed a talent for portraits and was fascinated with painterly methods of rendering light. He later called his years at the Art Institute his "utopia": "His dedication and ability garnered high marks and opportunities for exhibition. From lunches at the renowned Berghoff Restaurant to torrid love affairs, Motley's student days were a heady mixture of hard work and pleasure."[257] Motley absorbed both the drawing skills of the older instructors and the avant-garde attitudes of the young progressive students. Largely due to the Arts Club of Chicago, the Windy City was remarkably hospitable to avant-garde art during the Jazz Age, and several modernists, such as Pablo Picasso, had their first American solo shows in Chicago (Picasso's was at the Arts Club of Chicago in 1923). Other artists who were shown in Arts Club exhibitions included Marc Chagall, Salvador Dali, Georges Braque, Jean Dubuffet, Georges Seurat and Henri de Toulouse-Lautrec.[258] Once Motley had graduated from art school in 1918, he was able to marry Edith Granzo, a White Englewood neighbor he had secretly been dating since high school. She was a great help to Motley's career, taking different jobs to allow him to pursue his painting.

Motley's first attempt to depict the variety of Black culture came in the form of portraits—works that exemplify the "dignity" and "integrity" that Motley described as characteristic of modern Black life. The first painting he exhibited professionally was a 1919 portrait of his mother. Motley was especially interested in Black subjects with various shades of color in their skin. When he was in his thirties, he painted three beautiful portraits of light-skinned Black women. Of the first of them, he said, "I have tried to show that delicate one-eighth strain of Negro blood. Therefore, I would say that this painting was not only an artistic venture but a scientific problem."[259]

Motley began attracting notice. His painting *Mending Socks* (1924), which depicted his eighty-two-year-old grandmother, was named the "best-liked painting" at a 1927 exhibition of American artists at the Newark Museum. When two of his paintings, *Syncopation* and *The Mulatress*, won cash prizes, the *Chicago Defender* proudly noted, "This is a signal honor for one of our number."[260] Motley's biggest step forward came with a one-man show at the New Gallery in New York, a nearly unprecedented feat for a Black artist. He sold twenty-two paintings and earned between $5,000 and $7,000 ($75,000 to $105,000 in today's money). The *New York Times* wrote, "In the portraits, Motley directly or by subtle indirection lays bare a generous section of what psychologists call the subconscious—his own and that of his race."[261] At the request of the gallery's owner, Motley had created five works based on African themes, but critics, even the critic from the *Defender*, were not that keen on them. But the exhibition also included three works that depicted Black music and dance—and these were popular. This was the new direction in which Motley was headed.

Motley went to Paris in 1929 for a one-year period of study as the recipient of a Guggenheim fellowship, bringing his wife and mother with him. He spoke some French, having learned the Louisiana Creole dialect from his parents (when he entered art school, he described himself as a "French Negro").[262] He sparsely partook of Parisian nightlife and showed little interest in the local creative community, including the American expatriate artists, musicians and writers.[263] He went to mass every Sunday and regularly visited the Louvre, soaking up lessons on, as he put it, "color, composition, technique, draftsmanship, and the effect of light."[264] He cited three artists in particular as his influences—Frans Hals, Eugène Delacroix and Jacques-Louis David.[265] But he spent nearly all his time in his studio, creating paintings "depicting the various phases of Negro life."[266]

It was in Paris that he created *Blues*. The setting of this painting is the Petite Café, a cabaret that attracted West Indians and Africans who were living in

France. The biracial atmosphere attracted Motley, and he later complained that American viewers at the time misunderstood the painting as depicting only Black people, as Americans were unable "to imagine a racially diverse gathering."[267] *Blues* was Motley's breakout work and "served as a template for some of Motley's most successful post-Parisian paintings."[268] *Blues*, the *Chicago Defender* said, created "a rather confused feeling of surprise, bordering on amazement.…There is no denying Motley's artistry."[269]

Motley returned to Chicago in full command of his powers. He had missed the city and declined an offer to extend his Paris stay. As he later said, "I feel my work is peculiarly American, a sincere personal expression of the age, and I hope a contribution to society.…The Negro is part of America and the Negro is part of our great American art."[270] Motley went on to paint a series of dynamic renderings of Black life that included *Tongues* (*Holy Rollers*, 1929), *The Plotters* (1933), *Black Belt* (1934), *Barbecue* (1934), *The Boys in the Back Room* (circa 1934), *Saturday Night* (1935), *The Liar* (1936), *The Picnic* (1936), *Carnival* (1937) and *The Jazz Singers* (circa 1937). The last of the series is the moody *Bronzeville at Night* (1949). Later in life, he returned to the genre with works such as *Barbecue* (1960) and *Hot Rhythm* (1961).

During the Great Depression, Motley was hired by the Works Progress Administration (WPA), a federal program that gave work to the unemployed, including artists. After the death of his wife, Motley took a job with Styletone, a manufacturer of hand-painted shower curtains, and in 1956, the *Chicago Tribune* ran a story titled "Top Negro Artist Works in Factory Job."[271] Calling Motley "one of the most distinguished Negro artists in America," the story noted that "his works have not brought him prosperity" and that he needed to "support his 86-year-old mother and a son attending DePaul University." Motley, the story said, considered his factory work "no tragedy": "Motley says he has had so many jobs that he cannot recall them all." In the early 1950s, Motley visited Mexico and produced a series of paintings based on Mexican themes. In 1980, he was one of the ten Black artists honored at the White House by President Jimmy Carter. Motley, who was then eighty-eight years old, could not make the trip and was represented by his son. He died on January 16, 1981. His obituary in the *New York Times* was a terse six sentences; his obituary in the *Chicago Tribune* was not much longer, but it did include a photograph of the artist at work.

When New York's Whitney Museum of American Art moved into its new building in 2015, its first one-man show was an exhibition of Motley's works. Soon after, the museum announced it had acquired its first work by Motley: *Gettin' Religion*. The museum's director said they had been "working

JAZZ ON CANVAS
Archibald Motley Jr. of
Chicago has been called "the
quintessential jazz painter."
Although his breakthrough
work, *Blues*, was created in
Paris, its inspiration was
the vibrant cultural life
of Chicago's Bronzeville
neighborhood. Blues, *1929 (oil
on canvas), Motley Jr., Archibald J.
(1891–1981), Private Collection,
© Valerie Gerrard Browne, Chicago
History Museum, Bridgeman Images.*

to bolster our holdings of works by key figures associated with the Harlem Renaissance, and the top of the list was bringing a major Motley painting into the collection."[272] It was a compliment to an understudied artist, but once again, Motley couldn't escape an association with the Harlem Renaissance, and his Chicago heritage was overlooked.

INVENTING THE SITCOM AND THE SOAP OPERA

The situation comedy, or sitcom, and the soap opera are hallmarks of American culture. Both were born in Chicago during the Jazz Age. As discussed in chapter 1, "Jazz and the Spirit of the Times," historian John A. Kouwenhoven has argued that "incompleteness" is a characteristic of modern American culture and that Americans favor an "open-ended" style. Viewed in this way, the sitcom and the soap opera are characteristically American. Both tell stories that are, or can be, endless. They, like jazz, rely on an aesthetic of incompleteness or arbitrary termination.

The airdate of the first sitcom was January 12, 1926. Not only was it the first sitcom, but it was also the most popular—ever. But it was peculiar and controversial, and today, it stirs discomfort. Its creators were pivotal in the creation of American broadcast entertainment, and they made Chicago the spearhead of the radio revolution, but no schools, parks or streets are named after them. The reason behind this is a Chicagoan story—an American story.

The first U.S. radio station to receive a federal license was KDKA in Pittsburgh, which began broadcasting on November 2, 1920. What followed was the development of a true mass culture; people across the United States began sharing the same experiences, absorbing the same ideas and, because of advertising, cultivating the same tastes and desires. Radio was crucial for putting the jazz into the Jazz Age. As radio sales rose, record sales declined, and by the mid-1920s, jazz fans were hearing their favorite music over the airwaves.[273] By 1924, there were 1,400 radio stations operating in the United States, and because of its central location, Chicago become a radio powerhouse. A powerful station broadcasting from the Windy City could be heard from the Rockies to the Atlantic. By 1925, there were some 40 radio stations in Chicagoland, and radio sets were selling briskly. In 1921, there were an estimated 1,300 radio receivers in the Chicago area; by the end of 1922, there were more than 20,000.[274]

Only second-rate stations played records; the classy ones hired singers, instrumentalists and bands, and the music was broadcast live. Stations also needed voice actors, comedians and writers, and among the many aspiring entertainers who came to Chicago in the early 1920s were Freeman Gosden and Charles Correll. Gosden, born in 1899, was from Richmond, Virginia, and Correll, who was nine years older, came from Peoria, Illinois.[275] Gosden and Correll worked for the Chicago-based Joe Bren Producing Company, which helped various organizations stage amateur musicals. Correll could play the piano, and Gosden could strum the ukulele; once the Bren Company assigned them to its Chicago headquarters, they worked up an act as a "harmony duo." In early 1925, they were hired by WEBH to broadcast as "Correll and Gosden, the Life of the Party." During one novelty number, they ad-libbed some dialogue in Black English. The bit went over well, and they expanded it, adding the voices of different characters. In October 1925, WGN hired them, and they became full-time radio performers, with the dialect skits becoming the foundation of their new act. As Gosden later explained, "We chose Black characters because blackface comics could tell funnier stories than whiteface comics."[276] Blackface comedy had been a prevailing form of American entertainment since minstrel shows began in the 1830s, but with the rise of radio, it was no longer necessary for a White comic to put on blackface makeup.

The situation comedy was born at WGN when Gosden and Correll premiered a show called *Sam 'n' Henry*. The nightly series followed the adventures of two young Black men from the South who had come to Chicago in search of a better life during the Great Migration. The skits told an ongoing story with characters who sympathized with the struggling and lampooned the pretentious.[277] As the series progressed, more characters (all voiced by Gosden and Correll) were added. Although racial stereotypes invariably arose, overall, the characters were sympathetic. The listeners were fascinated. After 586 broadcasts, Gosden and Correll's contract with WGN expired, and they signed with WMAQ. WGN still owned the *Sam 'n' Henry* show and hired replacement actors, which made it necessary for Gosden and Correll to develop new characters. Thus, *Amos 'n' Andy* was born on February 25, 1928.

Amos 'n' Andy became the most popular program in the history of radio broadcasting. The population of the United States in 1928 was about 120 million; once *Amos 'n' Andy* went national at the end of that year, the fifteen-minute program was attracting 40 million listeners nightly. By 1930, the show was a national hit. When owners of movie theaters found their seats half empty at 7:00 p.m., they would pipe in *Amos 'n' Andy*. The playwright

INVENTORS OF THE SITCOM
It was in Jazz Age Chicago that Freeman Gosden (*left*) and Charles Correll (*right*) created *Amos 'n' Andy*, the first situation comedy. *Courtesy of the University of Southern California.*

George Bernard Shaw said, "There are three things I'll never forget about America—Niagara Falls, the Rocky Mountains and *Amos 'n' Andy*."[278]

Many White listeners clearly liked the show because it reinforced their notions of superiority by emphasizing stereotypes of Black people. Yet the evidence indicates White audiences came to value the show's depth of character, its story lines and the characters' working-class identification. In addition, Black listeners were big fans. On August 20, 1931, when the *Chicago Defender* held its annual Bud Billiken Parade, Gosden and Correll were the guests of honor. As the *Defender* reported, when the band struck up the *Amos 'n' Andy* theme song, "The crowd went wild—they did—they did."[279]

One reason Black Americans accepted *Amos 'n' Andy* was that the humor was not condescending. As characters, Amos and Andy had their faults, but their problems were familiar. Also, many other characters in the program were successful and admirable. According to one historian, the show "not only acknowledged the existence of an educated, prosperous Black middle class, but the new series also made members of that class integral players in the continuing story."[280] Through *Amos 'n' Andy*, many White listeners discovered a strong Black community that they barely knew existed. And Amos and Andy, though comical, displayed striking moments of pride and dignity. In one episode, for example, Andy explained his dislike for his employer: "I don't want nobody callin' me 'boy, do dis' an' 'boy, do dat.' My name is Andrew H. Brown."[281] During the Depression, White audiences could relate to the duo's struggles with hardship and unemployment. As historian Rob Kapilow put it, "the program managed to transcend its own racist, minstrel-show stereotypes through characterizations of Black people of real depth and humanity that emphasized universal values of friendship and hard work."[282] Late in life, Correll said, "I don't think Blacks as a body resented the program. That certainly wasn't what we intended, nor did we ever feel it when we were on the air."[283]

For most of its radio existence, *Amos 'n' Andy* was a fifteen-minute nightly broadcast. Gosden and Correll wrote the scripts in a small office in the Palmolive Building and broadcast from the WMAQ studio in the Merchandise Mart. In 1943, the show was extended to half an hour and was broadcast only once a week. By the early 1950s, television was becoming the predominant home entertainment medium, and many radio shows moved to TV. An all-Black cast was hired, and the first broadcast of the *Amos 'n' Andy* television show was aired on June 28, 1951, during the annual convention of the NAACP, the nation's largest civil rights organization. The delegates unanimously endorsed a resolution that the program depicted "the Negro and other minority groups in a stereotyped and derogatory manner" and urged the show's cancellation. (The *Amos 'n' Andy Music Hall* radio show was still on the radio, but the NAACP apparently had no problem with it.[284]) Sponsors for the show became hard to find, and CBS cancelled the program after its second season.

Like the first sitcom, the airdate of the first soap opera can be stated precisely: October 20, 1930. And like *Amos 'n' Andy*, it was first aired on WGN. *Painted Dreams* was the creation of Irna Phillips, who was born in Chicago in 1901. As a youngster, she had theatrical ambitions, but her teachers advised her that she didn't have the looks. After graduating from the University of Illinois and doing graduate work at Northwestern and Wisconsin Universities, she worked as a teacher in Ohio. She came back to Chicago to attend a christening and dropped by WGN almost on a whim. Her appearance didn't matter in radio; an audition at the station went well, and she was given an unpaid position. Phillips and another actress worked up a little chat show about two women named Sue and Irene. The station's management put Phillips on the payroll and asked her to develop a serial aimed specifically at women.[285]

The result was the fifteen-minute-long *Painted Dreams*, universally acknowledged as the first soap opera. It was broadcast six times a week, and Phillips wrote every word. The series told the story of a Chicago-based Irish American family headed by a kindly widow named Mother Moynihan. Phillips played both Mother Moynihan and her boarder, Sue Morton. The other members of the cast were Mother Moynihan's friends, her grown children and her dog, Mike (also voiced by Phillips). Much of the story line revolved about the widow's efforts to ensure her children's happiness. As one historian put it, "The simple message of the drama was that marriage, love and motherhood offered the greatest achievement and destiny any female could hope to experience."[286] In 1932, Phillips told WGN that she wanted to bring *Painted Dreams* to a network and broadcast it nationwide. WGN insisted that the station owned the show. So, Phillips left WGN and filed a lawsuit in which her attorneys argued that she had never given the station the rights to her creation. The case dragged on until 1941, when the Illinois Supreme Court decided that Phillips had been "a salaried employee" of WGN and that the station owned the program.[287]

By 1941, however, Irna Phillips had become the "queen of the soaps," or, as one newspaper critic phrased it, "high priestess of the washboard weepers."[288] In 1957, she was on the cover of *TIME*. Among the other soap operas she either created or scripted were *Today's Children*, *Woman in White*, *The Brighter Day*, *The Road to Happiness*, *The Guiding Light* and *As the World Turns*.[289] At her peak in the early 1940s, Phillips had no fewer than five serials on the air, was writing 2 million words a year and was making $250,000 annually (nearly $4 million today). In all, she created or cocreated eighteen radio and television serials.[290] In 1954, she persuaded her sponsor to extend the length of *The Guiding Light* from fifteen minutes (then the standard length of a soap opera) to half an hour, thus proving that the genre could support shows of a greater scope. Although she spent much of her time in New York and California, she always considered Chicago her home and died in her house at 1335 North Astor Street on December 23, 1973.

By the time of Phillips's death, Chicago's pioneer broadcasting days were nearly over. One other great radio sitcom had come out of the city—*Fibber McGee and Molly* (1935)—but broadcast dramas and comedies had moved to television. Chicago produced significant innovations in TV's early days, such as the children's show *Kukla, Fran and Ollie* and *Garroway at Large*, which morphed into the *Today* show. But by the early 1970s, production had mostly moved to the spacious studios of California and New York.

INTERLUDE: HARRY KEELER'S NAUGHTY MAGAZINE

A Chicago-based magazine, Hugh Hefner's *Playboy*, played a major role in the sexual revolution of the 1960s. But another Chicago magazine, now forgotten, played an equally large role in the nation's first sexual revolution. It was called *10 Story Magazine*, and its editor was Chicagoan Harry Stephen Keeler.

Men's magazines featuring women in various stages of undress have existed since the *Police Gazette* (1845–1932).

The pictures in that magazine were drawings, but photographs of nude models began to appear around World War I. In the 1920s, some of these magazines, also known as "sex pulps," purported to be focused on "art," with names like *Artists and Models* and *French Art Classics*. Keeler felt no need for such pretense.

10 Story Book, November 1927. *Author's collection.*

Keeler (1890–1967) was born, lived and died in Chicago. He wrote around one hundred novels, some quite long and some best sellers, with elaborate plots and ingenious mysteries.[291] *10 Story Magazine* had been founded in 1901, but it wasn't until Keeler became its editor in 1919 that it became a girlie magazine. Keeler purchased many of the magazine's risqué pictures from foreign photography agencies. His favorite model was the mysterious Countess Vera Martin de Mueller (who was born in Iowa). For the stories, Keeler paid his writers all of six dollars. The jokes probably weren't funny, even in the Jazz Age: "Example of married man getting last word: 'Very well, then, here's the money.'" The publication's advertisements offer a unique insight into the mentality of the Jazz Age male: many were for "girl pictures," but others were for sex books, cartoon books, lonely hearts clubs and advice on how to conquer tobacco or morphine addiction or to shed fat.

10 Story Book lasted until 1940—an impressive run. Once, when Keeler was interviewed, he said he had no idea why the magazine was a success. But his answer was right there on the masthead: it was "A Magazine Devoted to Girl Pictures and Intriguing Stories."

GAMES WITH A JAZZ BEAT

Chicago Sports in the Golden Age

The 1920s are often called the "Golden Age of Sports" in the United States. The era produced legendary, game-changing stars like Babe Ruth (baseball), Jack Dempsey (boxing), Red Grange and Knute Rockne (football), Bobby Jones (golf), Johnny Weissmuller (swimming), Big Bill Tilden and Helen Wills (tennis) and at least one animal—Man O' War (horse racing).

Can it be said that these athletes somehow embodied the jazz moderne spirit of the times? Many thought so at the time and still do. These stars played with a fresh flamboyance and excitement. As mass-circulation newspapers, live radio broadcasts and movie newsreels turned athletes into national figures, sports became both popular and lucrative. America's obsession with sports had begun.[292]

The Bear Who Saw a Ghost

Football was tremendously popular in Jazz Age Chicago. But it was the college game, not professional football, that was a hit. The sport's major celebrity was Coach Knute Rockne of Notre Dame, who gave America the "Gipper" and the "Four Horsemen." As the *Chicagoan* magazine put it in 1928, "very plainly, there is one university whose football activities are a matter of genuine interest and concern to the man in the street— Notre Dame."[293] Also, in the Jazz Age, the University of Chicago, led by the illustrious coach Amos Alonzo Stagg, won two national and eight Big Ten titles (the first Heisman Trophy winner, Jay Berwanger, played for the University of Chicago), and Northwestern University tied for the Western Conference title in 1926, 1930 and 1931.

But then came Chicagoan George Stanley Halas, born in 1895 in the Pilsen neighborhood to emigrants from what is now the Czech Republic. At the University of Illinois, he played baseball, basketball and football while earning an engineering degree. After serving a year in the navy during World War I, he signed on with the New York Yankees, but a hip injury ended his baseball career (it didn't help that his batting average was .091). He returned home and got a job designing railroad bridges.

In 1920, professional football had been around for about twenty-five years, but it existed mostly in small towns, where the players were paid per game; no organized national league existed. In August 1920, Ralph Hay, the owner of the Canton Bulldogs, met with three other professional team owners and formed the American Professional Football Conference. A month later, the group expanded to include ten teams, one of which was the Decatur Staleys, named after the Illinois corn-processing firm A.E. Staley. Halas became head coach in 1920 and recruited top-flight athletes, the most impressive of whom was center George "The Brute" Grafton, whose nickname signifies the type of players Coach Halas favored.[294] According to Halas's biographer Jeff Davis, the Staleys were experts at "tripping, kneeing, elbowing, slugging, gouging, biting, and, most important, the art of holding."[295] The team was, to use a word often used to describe Halas, ruthless.

Staley was proud of his team, but they were getting to be unaffordable. He proposed that Halas take over and move the team to Chicago. Halas quickly made a deal with the Chicago Cubs to rent Wrigley Field for football games. Already a big Cubs fan, Halas regarded football players as meaner and bigger than baseball players, so he renamed the team the Bears. At the spring 1922 meeting of the American Professional Football Association, Halas complained that the word *association* had a second-class ring to it and proposed a new designation: National Football League (NFL). The other owners agreed.

Halas's greatest coup in the Bears' early years was his signing of the college football superstar of the Jazz Age—Harold Edward "Red" Grange of Wheaton, Illinois. After scoring seventy-five touchdowns in high school, Grange went to Halas's alma mater, the University of Illinois. To Grange belongs the distinction of having given what was arguably the greatest one-day performance in the recorded history of sport. It came on October 18,

1924, when Illinois hosted Michigan in the new University of Illinois Stadium. Grange returned the opening kickoff for a ninety-five-yard touchdown. In the next twelve minutes, he scored three more touchdowns on runs of sixty-seven, fifty-six and forty-four yards. He was getting a little worn out, so Halas put him on the bench until the third quarter, when Grange scored touchdown number five on a twelve-yard run. To top it off, in the final quarter, he passed for twenty-three yards and another touchdown for a final score of 39–14. And this was against a defense that had given up only three touchdowns in its last two seasons.

Films of Grange show he was a shifty runner who moved with a fluid, deer-like motion and could instantly change speeds or even come to a dead stop to make tacklers miss. His college coach, Bob Zuppke, devised a more open style of football, contrary to the defensive game that was then in vogue. In a sense, Grange changed football as much as Ruth changed baseball—he gave life to an overlooked facet of the game. Sportswriter Grantland Rice gave the star a new nickname that replaced "Iceman"—the "Galloping Ghost."

BIRTH OF THE NFL
When George Halas of Chicago signed collegian Harold "Red" Grange to play professional football, he ensured the success of the Bears—and the National Football League. *Author's collection.*

Red Grange played his first game for the Bears on Thanksgiving Day in 1925 against the Chicago Cardinals. The match ended with a 0–0 score, but it drew thirty-six thousand spectators. "I knew then and there," said Halas, "that pro football was destined to be a big-time sport."[296] He was right. Sportswriters began paying attention to professional football—and their interest didn't waver after Grange retired. Grange was instrumental in the success of the NFL establishing franchises in large cities rather than the mid-size burgs it had been playing in.[297]

THE "HARLEM" GLOBETROTTERS

It's understandable that people would assume that the famous Harlem Globetrotters basketball team came from New York City, but the squad is as Chicagoan as the Wrigley Building. It's as Chicagoan as Abe Saperstein.

While George Halas was creating the NFL, another Chicago professional sports entrepreneur put the jazz spirit into basketball. Abe Saperstein was the son of Jewish emigrants from Poland. Although he was barely over five feet tall, Saperstein played a slew of sports at Lake View High School—baseball, football, basketball, boxing and track. Even so, he realized that his size made a serious athletic career unlikely for him and that his future lay in coaching.

Like professional football, professional basketball was slow to catch on in America. One of the first to make it work was Saperstein, who, in 1926, was offered the job of coaching an all-Black American Legion team. Because they played in the Savoy Ballroom on the South Side of Chicago, he called the team the Savoy Big Five. The Savoy operation went bust over money, and in 1927, Saperstein decided to turn his squad into a barnstorming team named the Harlem Globetrotters. Why Harlem? Because it identified the players as Black. Also, calling them the Bronzeville Globetrotters, which is what they were, wouldn't have given them the same name recognizability.

RIGHT TEAM, WRONG NAME
Despite their name, the world-famous "Harlem" Globetrotters were purely Chicagoan, created in the Jazz Age by a Windy City kid named Abe Saperstein. *Courtesy of the New York Public Library.*

According to his 1966 obituary in the *Chicago Tribune*, "For the Negro athlete, Saperstein was the basketball equivalent of Branch Rickey. He championed the cause of the Negro athlete long before Rickey brought Jackie Robinson into major-league baseball."[298]

Early in the team's existence, Saperstein added comedy routines to their performances, which have since become the hallmark of the team. But the hijinks didn't get in the way of excellence. According to a 1940 article in the *Chicago Tribune*, "over a 13-year span, [the Globetrotters] have won 1,710 games and lost 128, for a winning percentage of .930."[299] In Chicago, in 1940, the team won the world's professional basketball tournament, proving that Black basketball players could compete at the highest level. In that year, a columnist for the Black-owned newspaper the *Chicago Defender* went so far as to write "basketball is NOT a White man's game. The pale faces just don't know how to play it."[300] In 1948, the Globetrotters defeated the great Minneapolis Lakers, 49–45, a game that has been credited with ending segregation in the National Basketball Association (NBA).[301] Ironically, once the NBA was integrated, the best Black players no longer saw the need to join a team that followed an exhausting schedule that demanded continuous travel around the world. The Globetrotters became an exhibition team, although a much-loved one. They have played on every continent, except Antarctica, and have been seen by more fans than any other sports team in history.[302]

The introductory chapter of this book cited the argument of historian Davarian L. Baldwin that "the jazz music accompaniment that drew fans to the unproven commodities of basketball and professional football directly influenced the style of play." He contended:

> [Black athletes] *helped cultivate a reactionary approach to sport largely premised on defense, speed, adaptation, and adjustment. Black style on Bronzeville playing fields was expressed through the slap-fist defense and counterpunch style of Jack Johnson; the elusive and deceptive misdirection football moves of Fritz Pollard and college standout Ossie Simmons; the fast-paced, defensive, base-stealing, pitching-oriented "thinking man's baseball" of Rube Foster and his Negro Leagues; and the speedy-dribble, fake-pass play of the Savoy Big Five, who later became the Harlem Globetrotters—never from Harlem, forever from Bronzeville.*[303]

THE CHICAGO AMERICAN GIANTS

Chicago's Major League baseball teams were not exactly roaring during the Roaring Twenties. The Cubs had once been great, but by the 1920s, the team had fallen on hard times: sixth place in 1920, seventh in 1921, fifth in 1922, fourth in 1923 and fifth again in 1924. They hit rock bottom in 1925, when they finished last, twenty-seven and a half games behind the Pittsburgh Pirates. The crosstown Chicago White Sox were also struggling. They had finished first in 1919 and second in 1920, but then they declined: the highest they finished between 1921 and 1933 was fifth. Even their greatest triumph was ruined. The year that they went to the World Series, 1919, was the year of the "Black Sox" scandal, in which eight members of the team were accused of taking bribes to throw the series.

In the Jazz Age, however, Chicago had a third professional baseball team, and they were outstanding—the Chicago American Giants of the Negro National League. Sports historian Paul Debono has written, "It is a wonder that the story of the Chicago American Giants hasn't been more widely circulated. The history of the Chicago American Giants is as vital to the subject of baseball history as, say, biology is to science."[304]

The first all-Black baseball league to last more than a few seasons was the Negro National League, founded early in 1920. It comprised eight Midwestern teams, two from Chicago. Its first president was Andrew "Rube" Foster, who had started his career as a talented pitcher and then moved into management. As the manager of the American Giants, the Texas-born Foster became one of the most prominent Chicago sports figures of the Jazz Age. He was known as the "Father of Black Baseball," and he made Chicago its national capital.

Foster's American Giants won the first Negro National League title in 1920, with a winning percentage of .777. They repeated as champions in 1921 and 1922 and did a lot to make the league a financial success. After the 1923 season, Foster's team played three exhibition games against the major-league Detroit Tigers. The first game ended in a tie due to darkness, and Foster's team lost the second 7–1, but the American Giants won the third game 8–6, proving that a Negro league team could compete with a team from the majors. After a second Negro league—the Eastern Colored League—was established in 1923, Foster formulated a "Colored World Series."

During the 1925 season, Foster was nearly asphyxiated by a faulty gas heater in an Indianapolis boardinghouse. The incident seemed to leave him with brain damage, and his management and behavior in general became erratic. Midway through the 1926 season, he went to Michigan to recuperate. After two weeks, he returned to Chicago, but his behavior became dangerous, and he was placed in the state mental hospital. "Gentleman" Dave Malarcher took over as manager, and the Chicago American Giants won the Colored World Series in 1926 and 1927. The Negro leagues suffered during the Great Depression, and when major-league baseball was integrated in 1947, the league went out of business. Meanwhile, Rube Foster saw none of this; he died in the asylum in Kankakee, Illinois, in 1930. No monument to Foster exists in Chicago, and the stadium in which the American Giants played burned down in 1940. The site is now a housing project.

THE CUBS REBUILD AND THE GREATEST SEASON EVER

Wrigley Field, the home stadium of the Chicago Cubs, was built in 1914, when it was known as Weeghman Park and belonged to the Chicago Whales of the short-lived Federal League. Its capacity then was only about eighteen thousand, but in the early 1920s, the park was expanded and renovated, and an upper deck was added in 1928. In 1926, it was officially renamed Wrigley Field after the chewing gun magnate William Wrigley, who had bought the team in 1920. As they were in the second decade of the twenty-first century, the Cubs were in rebuilding mode in the Jazz Age, and William Veeck, the club's president, hired a new manager named Joe McCarthy, who turned out to be one of the greatest managers in the sport's history.

The team already had two valuable assets: catcher Gabby Hartnett and first baseman Charlie Grimm. Then the other pieces began to fall into place—gifted left fielder Riggs "Old Hoss" Stephenson, pitchers Charlie Root and Guy Bush and shortstop Woody English. Then came pitchers Hal Carlson and Pat Malone and Baseball Hall of Fame outfielder Kiki Cuyler. McCarthy's greatest coup, however, was his acquisition of one Lewis "Hack" Wilson, a fearsome slugger. Sparky Adams, an infielder for the St. Louis Cardinals, once recalled, "Hack could hit a ball with his eyes shut, and he hit it a long way. I have a mark on my shins yet."[305]

Lewis Wilson, who was born in Elwood City, Pennsylvania, on April 26, 1900, stood five feet, six inches tall and weighed 195 pounds. Today, his body mass index (BMI) would be 31.47, which is considered obese; this goes to show the value of measuring BMI. Wilson had colossal neck and shoulder

"HE AIN'T GOT NO NECK"
Standing five feet, six inches tall and weighing 195 pounds, Hack Wilson of the Chicago Cubs didn't look like anyone's idea of a baseball player, but he could hit the ball and send it flying for a mile. The Jazz Age gave birth to the idea of athletes' endorsements, and Hack had his own line of wagons for kids. Chicago-based Radio Flyer led the way in adapting Art Deco designs for household items. *Author's collection.*

muscles. He had an eighteen-inch neck and wore size six shoes. Wilson was surprisingly fast; he played centerfield, not a position for the sluggish.

In the minor leagues, Wilson not only hit a lot of home runs, but he also sported a high batting average (.388 in 1922), and by the fall of 1923, he was in the majors with the New York Giants. He never quite earned the approval of manager John McGraw, who couldn't accept that a player with such an odd build could succeed. Of Wilson, he said, "He ain't got no neck."[306] When Wilson struggled early in the 1925 season, the Giants sent him to the minor-league Toledo Mud Hens, and when he became available in the minor-league draft, McCarthy grabbed him.

The Cubs then began their ascent from the cellar: fourth in 1926 and 1927 and third in 1928. Then, before the 1929 season, the team acquired Baseball Hall of Famer Rogers Hornsby, who had batted .387 in 1928. (In 1924 he hit .424.) Wilson's stats rose with his team—21, 30, 31 home runs— until, in 1929, he clobbered 39 homers, batted in 159 runs and batted .345. People started comparing him to Babe Ruth.[307] (Like Ruth, Wilson was a world-class boozer.)

In 1929, the Cubs finally won the pennant. The World Series saw them matched against the intimidating Philadelphia Athletics (As), the winners of 104 games during the regular season. The first two games of the series were played at Wrigley Field, and the As took both. The Cubs got back into contention with a 3–1 victory in Philadelphia, but then came the memorable fourth game. The Cubs were cruising into the bottom of the seventh inning with an 8–0 lead when the leadoff hitter, Al Simmons, smacked a home run that was fair by inches. After Jimmie Foxx singled, Bing Miller lifted a soft fly ball to center, but Wilson couldn't catch it because the sun blinded him. It was another single. Three more singles, and the score was 8–4; two men were on, and McCarthy brought in a new pitcher. Mule Haas then poked a catchable fly out to Wilson, and he lost the ball in the sun again. It was an inside-the-park home run, and the score was 8–7. The nightmare continued, as the A's pushed across another three runs and eventually won, 10–8. McCarthy told a reporter, "I'll never believe what my eyes saw in that bad dream Saturday."[308] In the fifth game, the As scored three runs in the bottom of the ninth to win the game 3–2 and the series 4–1. Although Wilson had batted .471 in the World Series, the two dropped fly balls were all the fans remembered, and poor Hack was razzed in Chicago as "Sunny Boy."

There was little reason to tease Hack Wilson in 1930. He put up a season for the ages, although he did get off to a slow start—in April, he had only four home runs and eleven runs batted in (RBIs). But then, Wilson started to heat up. Between May 4 and May 10, he had fourteen RBIs in six games and had raised his batting average to .353. Between April 25 and May 20, Wilson went on a twenty-two-game hitting streak, hit ten homers, knocked in twenty-eight runs and batted .442. By the first week of June, the entire team was hot, scoring a startling seventy-two runs in five games, during which Wilson batted .440.[309] By this point, Wilson was becoming an RBI machine. On June 1, he batted in five runs against the Pirates. On June 23, in a game against the Phillies, Hack hit for the cycle and batted in five runs again. He had five RBIs on July 26, four on August 10, four again on August 18 and August 26, six on August 30, four on September 6, six once more on September 12 and four on September 17 and 27.

When, on September 17, 1930, Wilson drove in four runs and brought his total to 177, he broke the major league record of 174 that had been set by Lou Gehrig of the Yankees in 1927. Ten days later, Wilson collected his fifty-fifth and fifty-sixth home runs, setting a National League record that stood until 1998. With those two homers, Hack raised his RBI total to 189. He would collect two more before the season ended.

Wilson finished the 1930 season with 56 home runs, 191 RBIs, a batting average of .356 and a league-leading slugging percentage of .723. Some sports historians have called Wilson's 1930 season the greatest ever by a baseball player. Statisticians who have crunched the numbers say it probably wasn't the best, just tremendously good. Wilson's RBI record has never been topped.[310] Baseball historians are reluctant to speak of records that will never be broken, but Hack's RBI mark seems pretty safe in today's era of relief pitching specialists.

The Cubs went to the World Series three times in the 1930s. Although they didn't win the whole thing, during the Great Depression, the Cubs were considered one of baseball's class teams, one that was always in contention and one that continued to draw a large annual attendance. But although the team prospered, Wilson did not. His statistics plummeted—in 1931, he had only thirteen home runs and sixty-one RBIs while batting a mere .261. The following year, the Cubs traded him to Brooklyn, and his career continued to decline. In his last season, in 1934, he appeared in just seven games for the Phillies. Wilson slipped into obscurity and died, mostly forgotten, in Baltimore in 1948; he wasn't inducted into the Baseball Hall of Fame until 1979.

But for that one shining moment, Wilson was the hero of Chicago. At least since the celebrated Columbian Exposition ("White City") of 1893, Chicago had been in competition with New York for all sorts of honors (skyscrapers, for example), and many Chicagoans predicted their city would eventually eclipse New York in population. For these civic boosters, Hack Wilson was Chicago's answer to Babe Ruth. If New York boasted a peerless slugger, at least for one glorious season, Chicago did, too.

The Fight of the Century

The most exciting sports event in Chicago in the Jazz Age might still be the most famous boxing match in history. It matched two elite heavyweights—William Harrison "Jack" Dempsey and James Joseph "Gene" Tunney, who waged their momentous battle at Soldier Field.

In the 1920s, newspapers gave enormous coverage to boxers—much more than they do today. Champion fighters, who ranked as A-list celebrities, were the highest-paid athletes in the world.[311] Films of their bouts brought huge audiences into movie theaters, and the fights were also broadcast live on the radio, drawing millions of listeners.

Ironically, at the beginning of the Jazz Age, Chicagoans were unable to see professional boxing matches of any kind. Professional boxing had been banned in the city since the mid-nineteenth century, although "sports clubs" held fights anyway—that is, until 1904, when Mayor Carter Harrison II cracked down on enforcing the anti-boxing laws.[312] Amateur boxing, however, was still permitted in Chicago; it was a loophole that enabled the city to make ring history in the early 1920s. In 1923, Arch Ward, a sports editor at the *Chicago Tribune*, proposed a citywide amateur boxing tournament. It was a success, with 424 boxers entering, and the winner of each division was given an award in the shape of a miniature golden boxing glove. Under the leadership of Ward, what became known as the Golden Gloves Tournament went international. The Golden Gloves of America Inc., born in Chicago, continues to promote amateur boxing in the United States and has been a springboard for such champions as Joe Louis, Muhammad Ali, Sugar Ray Leonard and Mike Tyson.

The ban on professional boxing was lifted in 1926, so although Jazz Age Chicago hadn't seen professional boxing in nearly a quarter of a century, the city had a vast fan base for the sport. It also had a huge new stadium called Soldier Field. Everything was in place for Chicago to host the "fight of the century."

In his early career, Jack Dempsey, who was born in Manassa, Colorado, on June 24, 1895, traveled on freight trains, hustling fights in different towns, where he specialized in knocking out barroom bullies, shocking cowboys who couldn't believe that a skinny kid with a high-pitched voice could uncoil such a lethal left hook. Dempsey acquired a reputation as a destroyer and cultivated a scruffy, three-day growth of beard to make him look malicious. As Dempsey's manager, Jack Kearns—known as "Doc" —led him through some two dozen fights before arranging a bout with heavyweight champion Jess Willard. At the time, Dempsey weighed about 185 pounds, while Willard stood six feet, six inches tall and weighed 235. When the fighters entered the ring, it hardly looked fair. A film was made of the fight, and it's painful to watch. Dempsey knocked Willard down seven times in the first round. Somehow, the blood-covered Willard, with a broken jaw, managed to last three rounds.

After defeating Luis Angel Firpo of Argentina in what remains one of the most exciting heavyweight fights ever, Dempsey took a three-year break from boxing, during which he split with Doc Kearns. The public was impatient to see him in the ring, and the promoter Tex Rickard arranged a fight with a young fighter named Gene Tunney. Dempsey thought Tunney, who had a reputation as an intellectual, would be a pushover. One of Dempsey's trainers supposedly dismissed the challenger by saying, "He reads books."

Tunney was born in Manhattan on May 25, 1897, the son of an Irish immigrant dockworker who had some experience as a boxer. Schoolyard bullies picked on the skinny kid, and his father decided to buy him boxing gloves and teach him self-defense. Tunney dropped out of school at the age of sixteen and became an office boy. He was, however, a perfect autodidact and read extensively, especially Shakespeare's works, so even though he never finished high school, he had a collegiate quality to him that caused many to dismiss his pugilistic ability. During World War I, Tunney joined the Marine Corps, and in 1919, he became the light-heavyweight champion of the American forces in France. Three years later, then a professional, he won the American light-heavyweight crown. Once he became a heavyweight, it became inevitable that he would be matched with Dempsey—the "Fighting Marine" versus the "Manassa Mauler."[313] The match took place in Philadelphia on September 23, 1926. Dempsey later admitted that he "was nothing like [his] old fighting self."[314] James P. Dawson, covering the fight for the *New York Times*, wrote Tunney was "a complete master, from first bell to last. He out-boxed and he out-fought Dempsey at every turn."[315]

There had to be a rematch—but where? Rickard knew Chicago had legalized professional fights, was willing to raise the ceiling on ticket prices and had a vast new stadium. In 1927, he told Don Maxwell of the *Tribune*, "Look at the territory Chicago can draw from for this fight! There'll be special trains from Cleveland, New York, Detroit, St. Louis, Omaha, and the Lord knows where. They're all a-coming. Yes, sir, Chicago is going to draw the biggest crowd any city ever had."[316] The Dempsey-Tunney rematch, held before a live crowd of 104,943, was the first $2 million gate

MANASSA MAULER
A school dropout at sixteen, Jack Dempsey of Manassa, Colorado, went on to fight Gene Tunney in the "Long Count" bout in Chicago—still the most legendary boxing contest in the history of the ring. *Courtesy of the Library of Congress.*

($2,658,660) for any entertainment event in history. The worldwide radio audience was estimated at 15 million.

At the beginning of the fight, the referee, Dave Barry, reminded the fighters of a new rule: "Now, I want to get this one point clear. In the event of a knockdown, the man scoring the knockdown will go to the farthest neutral corner. Is that clear, Jack? Is that clear, champ?" He even said he wouldn't start the countdown until the man standing was in the corner.[317] Late in the fourth round, the champ opened a cut near Dempsey's right eye; then in the fifth, he staggered him with two rights to the jaw. The seventh round was the one for historians. Dempsey hit Tunney with a left hook, then a right and then, as Tunney came off the ropes, another—and mightier— left hook. Down went the champ. Dempsey went to the nearest corner, but it wasn't a neutral corner. Barry told him to move, but Dempsey didn't until Barry pushed him into a neutral corner. Five seconds had elapsed before Barry returned to the fallen Tunney and shouted, "One!" Tunney got up just before the referee reached ten—the most famous fourteen seconds in the history of American sports. Tunney dominated the final three rounds and won a unanimous decision.

Tunney had had fourteen seconds to recover—the so-called "long count." Could he have gotten up in ten? Tunney later said he could have been on his feet in two but realized it was best to take his time. Ringside observer Nat Fleischer, editor of the *Ring* magazine, believed Tunney was out at four but not at ten.[318] Barry thought the same. A film of the fight exists, but viewers can't see into Tunney's glassy eyes.

The irony of the fight is that Dempsey went into retirement not just admired but beloved—a celebrity on par with the other sports heroes of the Jazz Age. He opened a restaurant in New York's Times Square, where he sat greeting customers until his death at the age of eighty-seven. He said that the "long count" was probably the best thing that ever happened to him. Tunney defended his title once and retired at the age of thirty-one. He married a socialite, settled on a Connecticut farm and raised four children, one of whom became a U.S. senator. He died in 1978. Boxing historians have since rated Dempsey one of the best—perhaps the greatest. The Fighting Marine, who was knocked down just once in his professional career—has been practically forgotten. And when his name surfaces, it's not because of his brilliant boxing skills. It's because of the "long count" in Jazz Age Chicago.

THE RAINBOW CITY AND
THE END OF THE JAZZ AGE

When Did the Jazz Age End?

The earliest likely date might be October 24, 1929, known as "Black Thursday," when stocks fell 11 percent, kicking off a chain of events that pushed the nation into the Great Depression. Exactly two years later, on October 24, 1931, Al Capone was convicted of tax evasion, another possible end date of the Jazz Age. But Prohibition was still in effect, and speakeasies were still operating. So, maybe its end date was March 23, 1933, when President Franklin D. Roosevelt signed the Cullen-Harrison Act, which allowed the manufacture and sale of certain low-alcohol beer and wines. The ratification of the Twenty-First Amendment followed on December 5, 1933, and Prohibition was dead—along with, we might conclude, the Jazz Age. Chicagoans, however, might want to extend the era a little longer and choose October 31, 1934, as its end date. That was the final day of Chicago's second World's Fair—an Art Deco extravaganza known as the Century of Progress International Exposition.

Waiting for the Sunrise

Ideas for a second World's Fair in Chicago (the first being the "White City" Columbian Exposition of 1893) began percolating among the city's power brokers as early as 1923, when a city planner named Myron E. Adams pitched the idea of a grand fair to commemorate the centennial of Chicago's incorporation as a village in 1833.[319] The success of the Philadelphia Sesqui-Centennial International in 1926 roused Chicagoans into action, and in 1927, Rufus C. Dawes, the brother of the U.S. vice president, was named chairman of the board for the fair. Lenox R. Lohr, who had experience as a military engineer, became the fair's director of operations. The choice of "progress" as the theme was fitting for the spirit of the age, when technology was steadily unveiling new wonders. Raymond Hood, the co-designer of the Tribune Tower, was, along with French-born architect Paul Philippe Cret, put in charge of the overall architectural look. Hood's visit to Paris in 1929 convinced him that Art Deco streamlined modernism was the thing to epitomize progress. The Viennese-born Joseph Urban was put in charge of the exterior color of the buildings and was responsible for the intense palette of paints, which brought the fair the nickname the "Rainbow City" (in contrast to the "White City"). Colored lighting provided by eight miles of gas-filled tubes heightened the multihued appearance.

The fair was conceived during prosperity but built during a slump. Although the Great Depression was felt nationwide, it was intense in Chicago, with its large manufacturing base. It's been estimated that only half of the workers employed in manufacturing in Chicago in 1929 still had jobs in 1933.[320] However, in 1933, it was possible to believe that the corner of the Depression had been turned. Roosevelt was inaugurated on March 9 and immediately began pushing through a flurry of New Deal legislation. The unemployment rate began to decline, and the economy began to grow. The fair's directors added to the theme of progress that of recovery—not through federal legislation, however, but through science. "You probably have heard over the radio that 'all the world is waiting for the sunrise,'" one fair official said. "A Century of Progress may be the business sunrise that the world is waiting for, and it will be a demonstration of the splendid strength and vitality of the city of Chicago."[321]

COMMERCE, SCIENCE AND SEX APPEAL

The interwar period was a time of enthusiasm for international fairs and exhibitions. Architecture historian Mike Hope has counted no fewer than fifty-six such fairs between 1920 and 1940, attended by as many as 1 billion people in all who were exposed to new styles of art and design, adding the Century of Progress Exposition "would perhaps play the single greatest role

A BRIGHT MOMENT IN A DARK TIME
The great 1933 Century of Progress Exposition, which stretched along the Lake Michigan shore from the planetarium all the way to Thirty-Ninth Street, was meant to be a "demonstration of the splendid strength and vitality of the city of Chicago." *Courtesy of the Library of Congress.*

of any of these fairs in the dissemination and spread of not just architectural styles but also the materials and methods of construction."[322] (The fair was crucial in the introduction of novel building materials, like Masonite and Celotex.) According to Lisa D. Schrenk, "No other building project in the United States during the early 1930s promoted modern architecture as broadly as the second Chicago's World's Fair."[323]

The opening day of the fair was May 27, 1933. The exposition stretched along the Lake Michigan shore from the Adler Planetarium south to Thirty-Ninth Street. In the jazz spirit of the times, things moving meant things were improving. As Lohr explained, "People like to see things go 'round. There is motion or the suggestion of movement—progress—in all exhibits."[324] The center was the Hall of Science, a modernist edifice capped by a 175-foot-tall bell tower. The design of its eight-acre interior was streamlined Art Deco, and it displayed a massive mural titled *The Tree of Knowledge.* Among the exhibits were a geological clock, a lifesize transparent man and a model of a molecule of salt. The building most represented on souvenirs and posters was the Travel and Transport Building by Holabird & Root, which had a vast "floating" roof suspended from surrounding derrick-like structures that some found hideous and others found revelatory. Chicago architecture critic Thomas Tallmadge called it a "spider."[325]

Many of the other structures were sponsored by corporations. The fair's organizers realized that public funds would never suffice to foot the bill and prevailed upon American businesses to spend the staggering sum of $32 million on buildings.[326] It is important to note the role major corporations played in the spread of the Deco-Streamline style. According to architecture historian Mike Hope, "It is perhaps with the corporate headquarters of

PANORAMA
OF
A CENTURY OF PROGRESS EXPOSITION
CHICAGO · 1933

companies and banks that Art Deco came to the fore, especially in the USA with a string of buildings in most major American cities."[327] It was in the corporate exhibits that fairgoers saw the most exciting examples of progress. In the General Electric Pavilion, visitors watched popcorn bursting in a microwave, and Westinghouse featured an X-ray machine and a robot named Willie that not only talked but smoked. In the AT&T Building, selected visitors could place a long-distance phone call to any of the fifty-four cities displayed on a huge electric map. Perhaps most revelatory was the display of television put on, surprisingly, by the Hudson-Essex Motor Company. At the popular General Motors exhibit, visitors (over 200,000 per day) could observe workers on two parallel assembly lines crank out a stream of Chevrolet Master Six automobiles—one every twenty minutes.

Despite the fair's emphasis on progress, for many, the most enduring image of the Century of Progress was not a futuristic home but a woman with no clothes on. She was Sally Rand, an unemployed movie actress and dancer who showed up at the fair's preopening party portraying Lady Godiva of medieval legend, riding a white horse and wearing nothing but body paint and a wig. The directors of the exposition realized that education was great but that fairgoers also wanted entertainment, so they allowed for amusement in an area called the Midway. Among the diversions were a flea circus, a roller coaster, live incubator babies, a freak show and the "Streets of Paris," which immediately hired Rand, whose Godiva stunt had caused a sensation. There, she developed her fan dance, in which she skillfully covered her body with fluttering ostrich feathers (until the end, when she lowered them). In the second year of the exposition, she added a bubble dance.[328] Rand's performance was not the only thing of an erotic nature at the fair. In "Visions of Art," for example, nearly naked demoiselles were bathed in colored lights, and in the "Life Class," patrons were given crayons and paper to "sketch" the nude models. The Midway also featured old-fashioned peep shows and strip shows, and at an entertainment venue called the Dance Ship, men could pay a fee to dance with a female partner and a bit more to get a

TECHNOLOGY IS TERRIFIC, BUT...
For many visitors to Chicago's Century of Progress Exposition, the most memorable display was not of some inspired new invention—it was fan dancer Sally Rand. *Author's collection.*

lot closer (the police closed this one down). There were plenty of complaints about all the salaciousness, and both Sally Rand and Dorothy Kibbee, a model in the Life Class, were brought before Judge Joseph B. David, who dismissed the case: "Some people would want to put pants on a horse....If a woman wiggles about with a fan, it is not the business of this court."[329] Such entertainments attracted the sporting crowd, and the organizers appreciated the financial advantages of having the fair stay open late.

In 1933, nothing symbolized progress more than an airplane. Chicago's Midway Airport (originally Municipal Airport) had opened in 1926, and in the following year, the young American flyer Charles Lindbergh completed the first solo flight across the Atlantic and became the most celebrated personage of the age. Chicago was a major incubator of aviation enthusiasm. Although the historic district on the near South Side known as "Motor Row" is now famous for its vintage automobile showrooms, in 1920, it also contained at least ten agencies that sold either airplanes or airplane motors. As one of the owners of those enterprises told a reporter, "Go to our remotely located flying fields, and you will find hangars filled with ships. There, too, you will find men and women who can fly the ships."[330] The Century of Progress Exposition featured many examples of aircraft, including the Texaco speed plane, in which Captain Frank M. Hawks had set a new transcontinental speed record, and a Boeing 247 passenger plane that was suspended from the ceiling of the Travel and Transport Building. At the beginning of July 1933, the city staged a series of "air races" that kicked off with a parade in the Loop. Later in the day, a show at Municipal Airport featured races, model planes, aerial acrobatics, parachutists and a flier who performed stunts with the motor turned off. As the newspaper reported, it was "a guaranteed hair raiser and spine chiller."[331]

By the late 1920s, airplanes were an established technology, but it was by no means certain that they were the best way to carry passengers through the skies. A competing technology—the dirigible, or zeppelin—was equally as promising. Zeppelins could then carry more than two dozen passengers on transatlantic voyages at eighty miles per hour.[332] The advantage of dirigibles over airplanes, it was thought, was that dirigibles could go much farther without landing or refueling. On August 28, 1929, the *Graf Zeppelin*, a massive German airship on a trip around the world, appeared over downtown Chicago as millions of cheering viewers mobbed the streets. The mighty ship, captained by none other than Dr. Hugo Eckener, the head of Luftschiffbau Zeppelin, the German firm that built it, circled the Tribune Tower, swung down to Soldier Field and then returned to Lincoln Park. The *Graf Zeppelin* was 776 feet long (a Boeing 747-98 jumbo jet measures 250 feet), and its appearance was one of the most dramatic sights ever seen in the Windy City.

In October 1933, Eckener brought the airship back to Chicago for a showing at the exposition. By this time, however, Adolf Hitler and the Nazis had come to power in Germany, and the airship then sported the Nazi swastika. For decades, the story was told that the anti-Nazi Eckener cleverly flew the zeppelin in a clockwise circle so that viewers on the ground could see only the starboard fins, which displayed the traditional German gold, black and red stripes, but historian Michael McCarthy, writing in *The Hidden Hindenburg*, has debunked this tale, presenting evidence that Eckener was happy to work with and endorse Hitler while also exploiting slave labor during World War II.[333] Another fascist regime, that of Benito Mussolini in Italy, also made an aviation sensation when the dashing General Italo Balbo, Italy's most famous flyer, flew his squadron of twenty-four Savoia-Marchetti SM.55X flying boats, which had come all the way from Rome, over Chicago on July 13, 1933. Mussolini also sent an ancient Roman column to the fair, and it was placed in front of the Italian Pavilion.

Because of the nation's aviation mania, the "Supreme Thrill of the Fair" was the Sky Ride. In 1933, few Americans had experienced a plane ride, and this ingenious contrivance allowed them to enjoy a comparable thrill—which they did in the amount of thirty-five thousand passengers per day.

"THE SUPREME THRILL OF THE FAIR"
The Sky Ride at the 1933 exposition featured aluminum and glass double-decker "rocket cars" that traversed the fairgrounds on cables 219 feet above the lagoon. *Author's collection.*

The Sky Ride featured aluminum and glass double-decker "rocket cars" that traversed the fairgrounds on cables 219 feet above the lagoon.

The fact that the conveyances in the Sky Ride were called "rocket cars" shows how the designers—and popular culture—were already looking ahead to space flight. The comic strip *Buck Rogers in the 25th Century A.D.* had debuted in 1929, and a similar strip, *Flash Gordon*, was first printed in January 1934, but a real-life spaceman was at the fair—Thomas "Tex" Settle of the U.S. Navy, a pilot of a balloon that was designed to fly into the stratosphere. The balloon's gondola had been designed by twin brothers Auguste and Jean Piccard, Swiss pioneers of high-altitude flight. The demonstration took place on August 5, 1933, when the balloon took off from Soldier Field before a vast crowd. It was bathed in searchlights, and its ascension was a "thing of great beauty."[334] But it went up one mile instead of ten and floated into a South Side railyard. Undaunted, Settle tried again the following November. This flight went from Ohio to New Jersey and set an altitude record of 61,237 feet. The *Century of Progress* gondola now hangs in Chicago's Museum of Science and Industry.

Auguste Piccard did not believe, however, that balloons were the future of high-altitude exploration. He predicted that one day, "giant planes" carrying five hundred passengers would fly "through the stratosphere at 500 miles an hour," and he also foresaw "rocket motoring" into space.[335]

The Century of Progress Exposition ran for two seasons. Its closing day was October 31, 1934, and some fairgoers came in Halloween costumes. The directors reported an attendance of 50 million, and even in the Depression, it made money. It was estimated that out-of-town visitors pumped $700 million into Chicago's economy, and according to one historian, the fair "played a significant role in initiating Chicago's economic revival, particularly for the city's building industry."[336] The fair also inspired other American cities (Dallas, San Diego, Cleveland, San Francisco and New York) to stage similar expositions. As the exposition closed, Rufus C. Dawes commented, "Were we to live a thousand years, we would never forget it, for it lifted up our spirits, restored our souls, and brought us hope. This exposition spoke to a world in distress, and it spoke with the authentic voice of Chicago, asserting pride and announcing faith."[337] The structures and exhibitions were quickly removed or demolished, and the only vestige that remained was Mussolini's Roman column, which stood as a lonely sentinel between Northerly Island and Soldier Field. The memory of the fair, however, was immortalized when Chicagoans made it the fourth star on the city flag.

TO THE EDGE OF SPACE
By the time of the Century of Progress Fair, Americans were already viewing space as the next frontier. Spectators gaped when, on August 5, 1933, a balloon that was designed by Auguste and Jean Piccard and intended to carry pilot "Tex" Settle of the U.S. Navy into the stratosphere lifted off from Soldier Field. *From Wikimedia Commons.*

Although no Century of Progress structures remain, a great deal of what the Jazz Age contributed to American life endures. The era's music, literature, art and architecture all continue to provide pleasure and inspiration. People hold *Great Gatsby* parties, and tales of cops and robbers furnish plots for novels, films and television programs. Visitors ride buses on crime-themed Chicago excursions. Art Deco architecture walking tours are now a staple of the Chicago Architecture Center, and collectors seek out consumer goods, posters and jewelry in the moderne streamlined style.

Nostalgia for the era appears to have developed swiftly, which is understandable, given the rigors of the Great Depression, which made the 1920s look positively delightful. It didn't take long for Depression-era Americans to realize they were living in a different time. The term *Roaring Twenties* came into use as early as 1935, and a movie of the same name appeared only four years later. One of the taglines for the film was "America's most colorful era." In 1960, a company called Baker's Plays published the *Roaring Twenties Scrapbook* for people who wanted to stage a "Roaring Twenties Revue." The book provided "blackouts, sketches, monologues, suggested staging and routining, patter, opening and closing numbers—all in the mad, nostalgic mood of this popular decade." Appropriate costuming included "helmet hats, tasseled skirts, racoon coats, bell-bottom trousers, and striped blazers." The nostalgia for the period has proved to have staying power. We, like the people of the 1930s, romanticize the Jazz Age as a time of high spirits, vitality and optimism.

CHICAGO TIMELINE

1919–1933

1919

Some ten thousand packinghouse workers in Chicago go on strike. (July 18)

In what has been called "the first major aviation disaster in the nation's history," a dirigible named *Wingfoot Air Express* crashes in downtown Chicago, killing thirteen people. (July 21)

A race riot, triggered by an incident at a Chicago beach, plunges the city into a weeklong uproar characterized by shootings and arson. It results in the summoning of the state militia. Thirty-eight people (twenty-three Black, fifteen White) are killed. (July 27–August 3)

Alphonse Capone moves from Brooklyn to Chicago.

The Great Steel Strike of 1919 begins as workers walk off the job nationwide. Chicago, a major steel town, is especially affected. (September 22)

The "Black Sox" scandal—eight players for the Chicago White Sox are accused of taking bribes to throw the World Series.

1920

Prohibition goes into effect. (January 16)

The Michigan Avenue Bridge opens. (May 14)

George Halas of Chicago forms his first professional football team—the
Staley Starchmakers (also known as the Decatur Staleys). The team
moves to Chicago in 1921 and is renamed the Bears in 1922.

The Chicago-based American Giants baseball team, led by Andrew
"Rube" Foster, wins the first championship of the Negro National
League.

Chicago's population is 2,701,705.

1921

The Wrigley Building, the first skyscraper north of the Chicago River,
opens. (April)

Field Museum opens. (May 2)

KYW, Chicago's first radio station, receives its operating license.
(November 15)

The Chicago Symphony Orchestra gives the premiere performance of
Krazy Kat: A Jazz Pantomime by Chicago composer John Alden Carpenter.
(December 23)

Paul Biese, Frank Westphal and Jimmy Steiger publish a song titled
"Toddle," giving Chicago its nickname as "that toddlin' town."

1922

Louis Armstrong arrives in Chicago to join King Oliver's band. (April 8)

The *Flapper* magazine is published in Chicago, making the city, at least
temporarily, the capital of "flappermania." (May–November)

The *Chicago Tribune* announces that the competition to design a skyscraper
in which to house its offices has been won by John Mead Howells and
Raymond Hood. (December 2)

F. Scott Fitzgerald coins the term *Jazz Age*.

At a meeting of the American Professional Football Association, George
Halas's suggestion that its name be changed to National Football League
(NFL) is adopted.

1923

Reform candidate William Dever is elected mayor of Chicago, replacing William Hale "Big Bill" Thompson and beginning a crackdown on organized crime. (April 3)

The White jazz band New Orleans Rhythm Kings makes a series of recordings for Gennett Records in Richmond, Indiana, with Jelly Roll Morton at the piano. (July 17)

1924

The jazz trumpeter Bix Beiderbecke records "Jazz Me Blues" with the Wolverine Orchestra. (February 18)

Archbishop George Mundelein of Chicago is named a cardinal of the Roman Catholic Church, Chicago's first. (March 24)

Johnny Torrio and Al Capone take over the town of Cicero by stealing the municipal election through stuffing ballot boxes, kidnapping election officials and intimidating voters. (April 1)

In an attempt to commit a perfect crime, Richard Loeb and Nathan Leopold murder fourteen-year-old Bobby Franks. They are saved from execution by defense attorney Clarence Darrow. (May 21)

President Calvin Coolidge signs the Immigration Act, a bill that severely cuts immigration from eastern and southern Europe and excludes virtually all Asian immigrants. (May 24)

Municipal Grant Park Stadium opens. A year later, the name is changed to Soldier Field. (October 9)

In a game against Michigan, Red Grange of Illinois returns the opening kickoff for a ninety-five-yard touchdown, and in the next twelve minutes, he scores three more touchdowns on sixty-seven-, fifty-six- and forty-four-yard runs. He runs for a fifth touchdown in the third quarter and passes for a sixth in the fourth. (October 18)

Dean, or Dion, O'Banion, the head of the Northside Mob, is gunned down by hitmen working for Torrio and Capone. (November 10)

The Union Stock Yard reaches its historical peak as 122,749 hogs arrive in a single day. (December 14)

The Coon-Sanders Orchestra moves to Chicago from Kansas City. Two years later, they begin broadcasting on WGN and win a massive national following.

1925

Johnny Torrio survives an assassination attempt. He soon turns over control of the Chicago Mob to Al Capone. (January 25)

L'Exposition internationale des arts decoratifs et industriels moderne is held in Paris, giving rise to the term "Art Deco," a style that becomes known in the United States as "moderne," "modern," or "jazz moderne." (April–October)

The Women's World's Fair opens in the Chicago Furniture Mart. (April 18)

Union Station opens. (May 16)

Goodman Theatre opens. (October 20)

1926

The situation comedy is born at WGN Radio in Chicago when Freeman Gosden and Charles Correll premiere a new show called Sam 'n' Henry, which later becomes Amos 'n' Andy. (January 12)

The 2,448-mile-long highway from Chicago to Los Angeles is assigned the number "66," and "Route 66" is born. (April 23)

Chicago's Municipal Airport, later named Midway, is dedicated. (May 8)

Chicago plays host to the first Eucharistic Congress of the Roman Catholic Church ever held in the Western Hemisphere. Some 300,000 people pack Soldier Field for what becomes known as the "Catholic World's Fair." (June 20)

In an attempt to kill Al Capone, Hymie Weiss's gunmen spray some one thousand bullets into the Hawthorne Hotel in Cicero. Capone is unhurt, and in three weeks, he orders a lethal hit on Weiss. (September 20)

Wacker Drive, named after Charles H. Wacker, the first chairman of the Chicago Plan Commission, opens. (October 14)

In an effort to make Chicago "the best lighted city in the world," 140 new extra-bright streetlights are installed on State Street. (October 20)

The newly formed Chicago Blackhawks professional hockey team plays its first game. (November 17)

The ballpark in which the Chicago Cubs play is officially named Wrigley Field. An upper deck is added two years later.

1927

William H. "Big Bill" Thompson is elected mayor of Chicago for the third time, ending William Dever's four-year reform movement. (April 5)

Buckingham Fountain opens in Chicago's Grant Park. (August 26)

Heavyweight boxing champion Gene Tunney defeats former champion Jack Dempsey in the famous "long count" fight at Soldier Field. (September 27)

Louis Armstrong records "Struttin' with Some Barbecue" in Chicago with the Hot Fives, one of the first instances in which he refined the jazz solo by transforming the concept of improvisation. (December 9)

The Savoy Big Five, an all-Black professional basketball team in Chicago, is renamed the Harlem Globetrotters by its owner/coach, Chicago native Abe Saperstein.

1928

Arch Ward, a sports editor at the *Chicago Tribune*, initiates the first official Golden Gloves Boxing Tournament. (March)

The construction of 333 North Michigan Avenue by Holabird and Root, considered Chicago's first Art Deco skyscraper, is completed.

1929

Seven members of Bugs Moran's gang are lined up against a wall in a Clark Street Garage and gunned down in what becomes known as the "St. Valentine's Day Massacre." (February 14)

The German dirigible *Graf Zeppelin*, on a worldwide tour, makes a dramatic appearance over downtown Chicago. (August 28)

In what is known as "Black Thursday," the U.S. stock market falls 11 percent, setting off a chain of events that plunges the nation into the Great Depression. (October 24)

Chicago's new opera house, designed by Graham, Anderson, Probst and White, opens with a production of *Aida*. (November 4)

Eliot Ness organizes the group of crime fighters that becomes known as the "Untouchables."

Chicago artist Archibald Motley Jr. moves to Paris and creates his breakthrough painting, *Blues*.

1930

The Chicago Crime Commission creates a list of twenty-eight of Chicago's most dangerous gangsters. Al Capone becomes "public enemy no. one." (April)

The Merchandise Mart, designed by Graham, Anderson, Probst and White, opens. At 4 million square feet, it's the largest building in the world. (May 5)

The Adler Planetarium, the first in the Western Hemisphere, opens. (May 12)

The Shedd Aquarium opens. (May 30)

The Board of Trade Building, designed by Holabird and Root, opens. (June 9)

Painted Dreams, the first soap opera in entertainment history, premieres on WGN Radio. It is the creation of Chicagoan Irna Phillips. (October 20)

Hack Wilson of the Chicago Cubs bats .356, hits 56 home runs and drives in 191 runs (still the Major League record).

Chicago's population is 3,376,438.

1931

Czech-born Anton Cermak is elected mayor of Chicago. (April 6)

Al Capone is convicted of tax evasion. He is sentenced to eleven years in federal prison. (October 24)

1932

The U.S. postmaster general lays the cornerstone for a new Chicago Post Office Building, which, when it is completed two years later, becomes the largest in the world. (May 23)

New York Yankee slugger Babe Ruth hits a home run in the top of the fifth inning in a World Series game against the Cubs at Wrigley Field. Decades of debate have not settled the question of whether Ruth "called his shot" by pointing at center field and hitting the next pitch there. (October 1)

1933

Chicago mayor Anton Cermak is shot while meeting President Franklin Roosevelt in Miami. He dies on March 6. (February 15)

The Century of Progress Exposition, Chicago's second World's Fair, opens on Chicago's lakefront. Its closing day was October 31, 1934. (May 27)

The Museum of Science and Industry opens in what was the Palace of Fine Arts at the 1893 Columbian Exposition. (June 19)

Baseball's first All-Star Game is played at Chicago's Comiskey Park. (July 6)

The Twenty-First Amendment to the U.S. Constitution is ratified, marking the end of Prohibition. (December 5)

In the first NFL championship game, the Chicago Bears defeat the New York Giants, 23–21, at Wrigley Field. (December 17)

NOTES

Introduction

1. Jonathan Mekinda, "Chicago Designs for America," in *Art Deco Chicago: Designing Modern America*, edited by Robert Bruegmann (Chicago: Chicago Art Deco Society, 2018), 31.

2. The use of the term *Art Deco* became widespread with the publication of *Art Deco of the 20s and 30s* in 1968 by the British art historian Bevis Hillier.

3. Mike Hope, *Art Deco Architecture: The Interwar Period* (Ramsbury, UK: Crowood Press, 2019), 9.

4. Michael Levy, *Murder City: The Bloody History of Chicago in the Twenties* (New York: W.W. Norton, 2007); Curt Johnson and R. Craig Sauter, *The Wicked City: Chicago from Kenna to Capone* (Highland Park, IL: December Press, 1994); Norman Mark, *Mayors, Madams, and Madmen* (Chicago: Chicago Review Press, 1979); Douglas Perry, *The Girls of Murder City: Fame, Lust, and the Beautiful Killers Who Inspired Chicago* (New York: Viking, 2010); Chriss Lyon, *A Killing in Capone's Playground: The True Story of the Hunt for the Most Dangerous Man Alive* (Holland, MI: In-Depth Editions, 2014); Richard C. Lindberg, *Gangland Chicago: Criminality and Lawlessness in the Windy City* (Lantham, MD: Rowman & Littlefield, 2015); Chicago Tribune Staff, *Gangsters and Grifters: Classic Crime Photos from the Chicago Tribune* (Chicago: Midway, 2014); John J. Binder, *Al Capone's Beer Wars: A Complete History of Organized Crime in Chicago During Prohibition* (Amherst, NY: Prometheus Books, 2017).

5. Hope, *Art Deco Architecture*, 95.
6. Carol Willis, "Light, Height, and Site: The Skyscraper in Chicago," in *Chicago Architecture and Design, 1923–1993: Reconfiguration of an American Metropolis* (New York: Prestel, 1993), 130.

Chapter 1

7. Howard Pollack, *John Alden Carpenter: A Chicago Composer* (Urbana: University of Illinois Press, 1995), 131; Edward Moore, "John A. Carpenter Provides Humor for Chicago Symphony," *Chicago Tribune*, December 24, 1921; Frederick Stock, conductor of the Chicago Symphony Orchestra, was a champion of Carpenter's music and performed it more often than the music of any other American composer.
8. To take one example, the historian Donald Miller wrote that *Rhapsody in Blue* marked "the first time jazz was played on the concert stage." (Donald Miller, *Supreme City: How Jazz Age Manhattan Gave Birth to Modern America*, [New York: Simon & Schuster, 2014], 511.)
9. Pollack, *John Alden Carpenter*, 131.
10. Richard J. Powell, "Becoming Motley, Becoming Modern," *Archibald Motley: Jazz Age Modernist* (Durham, NC: Nasher Museum of Art at Duke University, 2014), 110.
11. Robert G. O'Meally, "Preface," in *The Jazz Cadence of American Culture* (New York: Columbia University Press, 1998), xi.
12. Kathy J. Ogren, *The Jazz Revolution: Twenties America and the Meaning of Jazz* (New York: Oxford University Press, 1989), 7.
13. Rob Kapilow, *Listening for America: Inside the Great American Songbook from Gershwin to Sondheim* (New York: Liveright Publishing, 2019), 227.
14. Quoted in Ogren, *Jazz Revolution*, 144.
15. Kevin Jackson, *Constellation of Genius: 1922, Modernism and All That Jazz* (London: Windmill Books, 2013), 400.
16. Lars Anderson, *The First Star: Red Grange and the Barnstorming Tour that Launched the NFL* (New York: Random House, 2009), 5.
17. Davarian L. Baldwin, "'Midnight was Like Day': Strolling Through Archibald Motley's Bronzeville," in *Archibald Motley*, 75.
18. John A. Kouwenhoven, "What's 'American' About America," in *Jazz Cadence*, 133–36.
19. Lawrence W. Levine, "Jazz and American Culture," in *Jazz Cadence*, 441–45.

20. David E. Kyvig, *Daily Life in the United States, 1920–1940: How Americans Lived Through the "Roaring Twenties" and the Great Depression* (Chicago: Ivan R. Dee, 2002), 10.

21. Robert J. Gordon, *The Rise and Fall of American Growth: The U.S. Standard of Living Since the Civil War* (Princeton, NJ: Princeton University Press, 2016), 130–31; Kyvig, *Daily Life*, 27.

22. Kyvig, *Daily Life*, 10–11.

23. Jon K. Lauck, *From Warm Center to Ragged Edge: The Erosion of Midwestern Literary and Historical Regionalism, 1920–1965* (Iowa City: University of Iowa Press, 2017), 54.

24. Kyvig, *Daily Life*, 71.

25. Kathleen Drowne, "Food and Diet," in *Encyclopedia of the Jazz Age: From the End of World War I to the Great Crash*, vol. 1 (Armonk, NY: Sharpe Reference, 2008), 242.

26. Joshua Zeitz, *Flapper: A Madcap Story of Sex, Style, Celebrity, and the Women Who Made America Modern* (New York: Crown Publishers, 2006), 55.

27. Ibid., 170.

28. Ibid., 168.

29. Miller, *Supreme City*, 209; Gerald Leinwand, *1927: High Tide of the 1920s* (New York: Four Walls Eight Windows, 2001), 174.

30. Miller, *Supreme City*, 173.

31. Leigh Kimmel, "Automobile Industry," in *Encyclopedia of the Jazz Age: From the End of World War I to the Great Crash*, vol. 1 (Armonk, NY: Sharpe Reference, 2008), 81.

32. Robert G. Spinney, *City of Big Shoulders: A History of Chicago* (DeKalb: Northern Illinois University Press, 2000), 174.

33. Along with *traffic jam*, another automobile-related term that entered the lexicon in the 1920s was *Sunday driver*. Meant to denote ineptitude, it described a person who didn't need their car for daily commuting but reserved it for pleasure on weekends.

34. Gordon, *Rise and Fall*, 2.

Chapter 2

35. Quoted in Bessie Louise Pierce, ed., *As Others See Chicago: Impressions of Visitors, 1673–1933* (Chicago: University of Chicago Press, 2004), 467.

36. John Drury, *Chicago in Seven Days* (New York: Robert M. McBride, 1928), 11.

37. Harvey Warren Zorbaugh, *The Gold Coast and the Slum: A Sociological Study of Chicago's Near North Side*, first printed in 1929 (Chicago: University of Chicago Press, 1976), 7.

38. In 1928, a group of real estate agents published, as a promotional tool, *A Portfolio of Fine Apartment Houses*, a large volume with illustrations of no fewer than eighty-three luxurious apartment houses that ran along the lakeshore from the Chicago River all the way to Evanston.

39. Irving Cutler, *The Jews of Chicago: From Shtetl to Suburb* (Champaign: University of Illinois Press, 1996), 69.

40. Irving Cutler, *Chicago: Metropolis of the Mid-Continent*, 4th ed. (Carbondale: Southern Illinois University Press, 2006), 47.

41. Miles A. Berger, *They Built Chicago: Entrepreneurs Who Shaped a Great City's Architecture* (Chicago: Bonus Books, 1992), 134; Willis, "Light, Height, and Site," 130.

42. Deborah Fulton Rau, "The Making of the Merchandise Mart, 1927–1931," in *Chicago Architecture and Design*, 99.

43. Harold M. Mayer and Richard C. Wade, *Chicago: Growth of a Metropolis* (Chicago: University of Chicago Press, 1969), 324.

44. Ibid., 294–96.

45. Mark J. Bournan, "'The Best Lighted City in the World': The Construction of a Nocturnal Landscape in Chicago," in *Chicago Architecture and Design*, 33.

46. Pierce, *As Others See Chicago*, 470.

47. James Langland, ed., *The Daily News Almanac and Year-Book for 1926* (Chicago: Daily News Co., 1925), 759.

48. Drowne, "Food and Diet," 1:243.

49. Neal Samors and Eric Bronsky, *Chicago's Classic Restaurants: Past, Present & Future* (Chicago: Chicago's Books Press, 2011), 60.

50. Drury, *Chicago in Seven Days*, 121.

51. "Artists' Colony Here May Rival Greenwich Village," *Chicago Sunday Tribune*, March 5, 1922, 4.

52. John Drury, *Dining in Chicago* (New York: John Day Co., 1931), 196.

53. Daniel R. Block and Howard Rosing, *Chicago: A Food Biography* (Lanham, MD: Rowman & Littlefield, 2015), 175.

54. "Tip Top Inn Surrenders to the Jazz Age," *Chicago Tribune*, September 13, 1931, 1.

Chapter 3

55. Robert G. Folsom, *The Money Trail: How Elmer Irey and His T-Men Brought Down America's Criminal Elite* (Washington, D.C.: Potomac Books, 2010), 58.

56. "How They Dish Out Hootch with Fish and Candy," *Chicago Tribune*, October 14, 1923, 3.

57. Neil Harris, "The Deluge: A Sounding of Chicago Prohibition," in *The Chicagoan: A Lost Magazine of the Jazz Age* (Chicago: University of Chicago Press, 2008), 61.

58. J. Anne Funderberg, *Bootleggers and Beer Barons of the Prohibition Era* (Jefferson, NC: McFarland, 2014), 37; William Howland Kenny, *Chicago Jazz: A Cultural History, 1904–1930* (New York: Oxford University Press, 1993), 153.

59. Folsom, *Money Trail*, 27.

60. Edward Butts, *Outlaws of the Lakes: Bootlegging and Smuggling from Colonial Times to Prohibition* (Holt, MI: Thunder Bay Press, 2004), 111.

61. Daniel Okrent, *Last Call: The Rise and Fall of Prohibition* (New York: Scribner, 2010), 259.

62. Butts, *Outlaws*, 107.

63. Daniel Francis, *Closing Time: Prohibition, Rum-Runners, and Border Wars* (Madeira Park, BC: Douglas & McIntyre, 2014), 25.

64. The Niagara Peninsula was nearly as active as the "funnel." (Francis, *Closing Time*, 11.)

65. Francis, *Closing Time*, 147.

66. Ibid., 157.

67. Edward Behr, *Prohibition: Thirteen Years that Changed America* (New York: Arcade, 1996), 175–76.

68. Okrent, *Last Call*, 141.

69. "2 Crowded Loop Speakeasies are Invaded by Drys," *Chicago Tribune*, June 12, 1929, 6.

70. Mary Murphy, "Bootlegging Mothers and Drinking Daughters: Gender and Prohibition in Butte, Montana," *American Quarterly* 46, no. 2 (June 1994): 176.

71. "Caldwell Blames Prohibition Law for Speakeasies Near City Public Schools," *Chicago Tribune*, November 23, 1928, 2.

72. David Rosen, *Prohibition New York City: Speakeasy Queen Texas Guinan, Blind Pigs, Drag Balls & More* (Charleston, SC: The History Press, 2020), 50.

73. Christine Sismondo, *America Walks into a Bar: A Spirited History of Taverns and Saloons, Speakeasies and Grog Shops* (New York: Oxford University Press, 2011), 216.
74. Behr, *Prohibition*, 185.
75. Nathan Miller, *New World Coming: The 1920s and the Making of Modern America* (New York: Scribner, 2003), 103.
76. G.K. Chesterton, *What I Saw in America* (New York: Dodd, Mead and Co., 1922), 144.
77. Bricktop, *Bricktop* (New York: Atheneum, 1983), 98.

Chapter 4

78. Michael Lesy, *Murder City: The Bloody History of Chicago in the Twenties* (New York: W.W. Norton, 2007), 267–303; Robert J. Schoenberg, *Mr. Capone: The Real—and Complete—Story of Al Capone* (New York: William Morrow, 1992), 128; Deirdre Bair, *Al Capone: His Life, Legacy, and Legend* (New York: Nan A. Talese/Doubleday, 2016), 74.
79. Harris, *Chicagoan*, 4.
80. Folsom, *Money Trail*, 60.
81. Lesy, *Murder City*, 267–68.
82. Binder, *Beer Wars*, 296.
83. Schoenberg, *Mr. Capone*, 179, 198.
84. Ibid., 189.
85. Bair, *Al Capone*, 10.
86. Roy Greenaway, quoted in Francis, *Closing Time*, 7.
87. Bair, *Al Capone*, 161.
88. The *Chicago Tribune* reported that in the late 1920s, Capone's gang had 181 members, only 75 of whom had Italian surnames. (Binder, *Beer Wars*, 62.)
89. Schoenberg, *Mr. Capone*, 177.
90. A map showing the gang territories is in Binder, *Beer Wars*, 66.
91. Bair, *Al Capone*, 76.
92. Binder, *Beer Wars*, 121.
93. Miller, *New World Coming*, 309; The other nine "outstanding personages" were Benito Mussolini, Charles Lindbergh, Admiral Richard E. Byrd, George Bernard Shaw, Bobby Jones, President Herbert Hoover, Mahatma Gandhi, Albert Einstein and Henry Ford. (Schoenberg, *Mr. Capone*, 242.)

94. Nate Hendly, *Al Capone: Chicago's King of Crime* (Neustadt, ON: Five Rivers Publishing, 2010), 100–2.

95. Douglas Perry, "The Truth About Eliot Ness," *Chicago Tribune*, January 24, 2014, 3.

96. Kenneth Tucker, *Eliot Ness and the Untouchables: The Historical Reality and the Film and Television Depictions* (Jefferson, NC: McFarland, 2000), 7.

97. Eliot Ness with Oscar Fraley, *The Untouchables* (Cutchogue, NY: Buccaneer Books, 1957), 43.

98. "U.S. Uncovers True Story of Capone's Rise," *Chicago Tribune*, June 14, 1931, 2.

99. Douglas Perry, *Eliot Ness: The Rise and Fall of an American Hero* (New York: Viking, 2014), 87.

100. Frank J. Wilson said that Ness's "love of notoriety severely limited his effectiveness." (Folsom, *Money Trail*, 90.)

101. The story of the Secret Six was pieced together and reported by Dennis E. Hoffman in *Scarface Al and the Crime Crusaders: Chicago's Private War Against Capone* (Carbondale: Southern Illinois University Press, 1993).

102. Luciano Iorizzo, *Al Capone: A Biography* (Westport, CT: Greenwood Press, 2003), 74.

103. The complete list can be found in *Scarface Al* (Hoffman, 111–12). Although the term *public enemy no. 1* is well-known, the Chicago Crime Commission, which has what might be called the naming rights, has used it only twice—first, for Capone, and then, in 2013, it bestowed the title on Mexican drug lord Joaquin "El Chapo" Guzman.

104. Binder, *Beer Wars*, 251.

105. Lucy Moore, *Anything Goes: A Biography of the Roaring Twenties* (New York: Overlook Press, 2010), 38–39; Hendly, *Al Capone*, 35–37.

106. Binder, *Beer Wars*, 289.

107. Ibid., 225.

108. Ibid.

109. David Witwer, *Corruption and Reform in the Teamsters Union* (Champaign: University of Illinois Press, 2003), 83.

110. Bair, *Al Capone*, 198.

111. Frederick Lewis Allen, *Only Yesterday: An Informal History of the 1920s* (New York: Open Road, 2015), 231.

112. Leinwand, *1927*, 142.

113. Howard Abadinsky, *Organized Crime* (Belmont, CA: Wadsworth Publishing, 2012), 68.

114. Folsom, *Money Trail*, 40.

115. Schoenberg, *Mr. Capone*, 199–200.

116. Quoted in Robert M. Lombardo, *Organized Crime in Chicago: Beyond the Mafia* (Urbana: University of Illinois Press, 2013), 18–19.

117. "Preachers Call O'Banion Rites Public Disgrace," *Chicago Tribune*, November 17, 1924, 2.

118. Genevieve Forbes Herrick, "Chicago Ne'er Had Funeral Like Genna's," *Chicago Tribune*, May 30, 1925, 1.

Chapter 5

119. Willis, "Light, Height, and Site," 128.

120. Katherine Solomonson, *The Chicago Tribune Tower Competition: Skyscraper Design and Cultural Change in the 1920s* (Chicago: University of Chicago Press, 2001), 1.

121. Joanna Merwood-Salisbury, *Chicago 1890: The Skyscraper and the Modern City* (Chicago: University of Chicago Press, 2009), 133.

122. "Announce Prize Plan for Tribune Home on Sunday," *Chicago Tribune*, November 22, 1922, 3.

123. "Late Foreign Prize Entry Stirs Judges," *Chicago Tribune*, November 30, 1922, 21.

124. Solomonson, *Tower Competition*, 84.

125. Jay Pridmore, *A View from the River: The Chicago Architecture Foundation's River Cruise* (Portland, OR: Pomegranate, 2000), 26.

126. "Howells Wins in Contest for Tribune Tower," *Chicago Tribune*, December 3, 1922, 1.

127. John W. Stamper, *Chicago's North Michigan Avenue: Planning and Development, 1900–1930* (Chicago: University of Chicago Press, 1991), 146.

128. Alice Sinkevitch, ed., *AIA Guide to Chicago*, 3rd ed. (Urbana: University of Illinois Press, 2014), 85.

129. Advertisement, *Chicago Tribune*, June 29, 1925, 3.

130. Wendy Kaplan, "'The Filter of American Taste': Design in the USA in the 1920s," in *Art Deco, 1910–1939*, edited by Charlotte Benton et al. (Boston: Bulfinch Press, 2003), 335.

131. Sharon Darling, *Chicago Furniture: Art, Craft, & Industry, 1833–1983* (New York: W.W. Norton, 1984), 273.

132. Eva Weber, *American Art Deco* (London: Bison Books, 1992), 8.

133. A detailed survey of this phase of the modern style can be found in Martin Greif, *Depression Modern: The Thirties Style in America* (New York: Universe Books, 1975).

134. John A. Menaugh, "Whole World Awheel Goes Streamline," *Chicago Tribune*, May 27, 1934, H1.

135. Jeffrey L. Meikle, *Design in the USA* (Oxford, UK: Oxford University Press, 2005), 113.

136. Bruegmann, *Art Deco Chicago*, 11.

137. Victoria Matranga and William E. Meehan Jr., "Anne Swainson: The Making of a Design Pioneer," *Innovation: Quarterly of the Industrial Designers Society of America*, Spring 2016, 20–25.

138. Pauline Saliga, "'To Build a Better Mousetrap': Design in Chicago, 1920–1970," in *Chicago Architecture and Design*, 265–66.

139. Mekinda, "Chicago Designs," 17.

140. Sharon S. Darling, "Skyscraper Furniture Suite," in *Art Deco Chicago*, 99.

141. On Faidy, see "After All These Years, the Recognition that Abel Faidy Longed to Achieve," *Chicago Tribune*, May 8, 1983, D-A2. For a photograph of an Art Deco bedroom designed by Faidy, see Edith Weigle, "Monotones Are Freely Used in Modern Decore," *Chicago Tribune*, October 21, 1934, C5.

142. Darling, *Chicago Furniture*, 277.

143. Ibid., 312.

144. Lisa D. Schrenk, *Building a Century of Progress: The Architecture of Chicago's 1933–1934 World's Fair* (Minneapolis: University of Minnesota Press, 2007), 157.

145. Paul F. Gehl, "When Chicago Led the Race for Modernist American Typefaces," *Chicago Art Deco Society Magazine*, summer/fall 2020, 14–16. See also Paul F. Gehl, *Chicago Modernism and the Ludlow Typograph: Douglas C. McMurtrie and Robert Hunter Middleton at Work* (Australia: Optifex, 2020).

146. WillElla De Campi, "The Home Harmonious," *Chicago Tribune*, April 22, 1928, F6.

147. Kathleen M'Laughlin, "Furniture Style Revue to Sound Modernist Note," *Chicago Tribune*, May 5, 1929, 22.

148. The prominent New York designer Paul Frankl even called his furniture and other fine art objects "skyscraper" style. (Drury, *Chicago in Seven Days*, 118.)

149. Brianna Rennix and Nathan J. Robinson, "Why You Hate Contemporary Architecture," *Current Affairs*, October 31, 2017, www.currentaffairs.org.

150. Hope, *Art Deco Architecture*, 57. The second was probably the "streamline" style.

151. Blair Kamin, "Chicago Motor Club Building, an Art Deco Gem, Revived as Hotel," *Chicago Tribune*, May 19, 2015, 14. Paul Alessandro, lead architect for the building's conversion, wrote an article titled "The

Rebirth of the Chicago Motor Club" (*Chicago Art Deco Society Magazine*, fall 2015, 25–27).

152. Cynthia Phillips, *Skyscrapers and High Rises* (New York: Taylor and Francis, 2009), 32.

153. See Werner Blaser, ed., *Chicago Architecture: Holabird & Root, 1880–1992* (Basel, CH: Birkhäuser Verlag, 1992).

154. Jay Pridmore, *The Merchandise Mart* (Petaluma, CA: Pomegranate Communications, 2003), 6.

155. The first building in Chicago to take advantage of air rights was Holabird and Root's Chicago Daily News Building (1929). For more information on the concept of air rights in Chicago, see Deborah Fulton Rau, "The Making of the Merchandise Mart, 1927–1931," in *Chicago Architecture and Design*, 104–8.

156. Tim Benton, "Art Deco Architecture," in *Art Deco*, 245.

157. Rennix and Robinson, "Why You Hate Contemporary Architecture."

158. For more information on GAPW, see Sally Kitt Chappell, *Transforming Tradition: Architecture and Planning of Graham, Anderson, Probst and White, 1912–1936* (Chicago: University of Chicago Press, 1992).

159. Robert C. Marsh, *150 Years of Opera in Chicago* (DeKalb: Northern Illinois University Press, 2006), 104.

160. Herbert M. Johnson, "The Chicago Civic Opera and Its New Home," in *Chicago: The World's Youngest Great City* (Chicago: American Publishers Corporation, 1929), 70.

161. Langland, *Daily News Almanac*, 898.

162. Charles Shanabruch, "Building and Selling Chicago's Bungalow Belt," in *The Chicago Bungalow* (Charleston, SC: Arcadia Publishing, 2001), 54.

163. Spinney, *City of Big Shoulders*, 175.

164. Dominic A. Pacyga, *Chicago: A Biography* (Chicago: University of Chicago Press, 2009), 220–22.

165. Joseph C. Bigott, *From Cottage to Bungalow: Houses and the Working Class in Metropolitan Chicago, 1889–1929* (Chicago: University of Chicago Press, 2001), 126.

166. For descriptions and pictures of bungalow kitchens, see Jane Powell, *Bungalow Kitchens* (Layton, UT: Gibbs Smith, 2000).

167. William E. Meehan Jr., "Hotpoint Toaster," in *Art Deco Chicago*, 140.

168. See Bruegmann, *Art Deco Chicago*.

169. Quoted in Steven Pinker, *Enlightenment Now: The Case for Reason, Science, Humanism, and Progress* (New York: Penguin Books, 2019), 252.

170. Pinker, *Enlightenment Now*, 251.

171. Miller, *New World Coming*, 150, 274–75.

172. Shanabruch, "Building and Selling," 70–71.

173. Leinwand, *1927*, 42.

174. Agnes L. Peterson, "What the Wage-Earning Woman Contributes to Family Support," *Annals of the American Academy of Political and Social Science* 143, no. 1 (May 1929): 74–93.

175. Bigott, *From Cottage to Bungalow*, 8–9.

176. In the summer of 2016, the Chicago Bungalow Association launched what it called its "Stop the Pop" campaign. Its aim was to halt the then-recent trend of adding full-sized second floors covered in siding, not brick, to bungalows. The association argued that the pop-ups were destroying the aesthetic and architectural values of the properties. Two years later, the association began a program ("Bungalow Expansion Project") that advised homeowners on how to increase bungalow floor space without adding complete second-floor additions.

177. Kristie Miller, "Yesterday's City: Of the Women, for the Women, and By the Women," *Chicago History*, Summer 1995, 58.

178. "Work of World's Women Shown at Chicago Fair," *Chicago Tribune*, April 19, 1925, 3.

179. "Women's Fair Adds Fame to Women's Art," *Chicago Tribune*, April 22, 1925, 25.

Chapter 6

180. Rick Kennedy, *Jelly Roll, Bix, and Hoagy: Gennett Studios and the Birth of Recorded Jazz* (Bloomington: Indiana University Press, 1994), 57.

181. Charles A. Sengstock Jr., *Jazz Music in Chicago's Early South Side Theaters* (Northbrook, IL: Canterbury Press of Northbrook, 2000), 9.

182. "Jazz Music at Pekin Pavilion," *Chicago Defender*, March 16, 1918, 12.

183. Quin Ryan, "Inside the Loud Speaker," *Chicago Tribune*, March 10, 1929, J11.

184. Quoted in Richard M. Sudhalter, *Lost Chords: White Musicians and Their Contribution to Jazz, 1915–1945* (New York: Oxford University Press, 1999), 11.

185. Ben Hecht, *One Thousand and One Afternoons in Chicago* (Chicago: Codicil-McGee, 1922), 223–26. It's highly doubtful that a jazz band had a bassoon.

186. Sidney Bechet, *Treat It Gentle* (Ann Arbor: University of Michigan, 1960), quoted in Robert Gottlieb, *Reading Jazz: A Gathering of Autobiography, Reportage, and Criticism from 1919 to Now* (New York: Vintage Books, 1996),

8; John Chilton, *Sidney Bechet: The Wizard of Jazz* (Cambridge, MA: Da Capo Press, 1996), 27.

187. Eddie Condon, *We Called It Music: A Generation of Jazz* (Cambridge, MA: Da Capo Press, 1992), 133.

188. Louis Armstrong, *Louis Armstrong in His Own Words: Selected Writings* (New York: Oxford University Press, 1999), 33.

189. Ogren, *Jazz Revolution*, 71.

190. Charles A. Sengstock Jr., *That Toddlin' Town: Chicago's White Dance Bands and Orchestras, 1900–1950* (Urbana: University of Illinois Press, 2004), 53.

191. William Toth, "Dance, Popular," in *Encyclopedia of the Jazz Age: From the End of World War I to the Great Crash*, vol. 1 (Armonk, NY: Sharpe Reference, 2008), 159.

192. Ogren, *Jazz Revolution*, 51.

193. "Jazz Music Held Obscene, Peril to Nation's Morals," *Chicago Tribune*, January 28, 1922, 5.

194. "Can You Toddle?—Better Learn—It's All the Rage," *Day Book*, December 29, 1916, 28.

195. Thomas Brothers, *Louis Armstrong: Master of Modernism* (New York: W.W. Norton, 2014), 31.

196. Martha, "Martha Seeks Why and What of Modern Dancing," *Chicago Tribune*, September 16, 1921, 17.

197. Martha, "Martha Plumbs Depths of Jazz North of the River," *Chicago Tribune*, September 18, 1921, 14.

198. Martha, "The Toddle Dies, Says Martha; To Mexatang, Hail," *Chicago Tribune*, September 10, 1921, 13.

199. "World's Famous Midway Gardens to Be Reopened," *Chicago Tribune*, September 4, 1921, F22.

200. Ogren, *Jazz Revolution*, 67–68.

201. Sudhalter, *Lost Chords*, 94.

202. Philip Furia and Michael Lasser, *America's Songs: The Stories Behind the Songs of Broadway, Hollywood, and Tin Pan Alley* (New York: Routledge, 2006), 40–41.

203. Harris, *Chicagoan*, 209.

204. Sengstock, *Toddlin' Town*, 11.

205. "Knife Relieves Obese Mr. Biese of Fifty Pounds," *Chicago Tribune*, February 12, 1920, 3.

206. Sengstock, *Toddlin' Town*, 150.

207. "Jazz Music is Immoral, Club Woman Asserts," *Chicago Tribune*, January 5, 1922, 17.

208. "Jazz Music Held Obscene," *Chicago Tribune*, January 29, 1922, 5.

209. "Charleston? Here's a Few Things It Will Do to You," *Chicago Tribune*, January 11, 1926, 1.

210. "Shimmy? Toddle? No Such Doin's in Our Schools," *Chicago Tribune*, January 18, 1921, 3.

211. Brothers, *Louis Armstrong*, 32.

212. John D'Emilio and Estelle B. Freedman, *Intimate Matters: A History of Sexuality in America* (Chicago: University of Chicago Press, 1997), 233.

213. Elmer T. Clark, *Social Studies of the War* (New York: George H. Doran, 1919), 34.

214. Simon Baatz, *For the Thrill of It: Leopold, Loeb and the Murder That Shocked Jazz Age Chicago* (New York: Harper, 2008), 321.

215. Maurine Watkins, "'Dick Innocent,' Loebs Protest: Plan Defense," *Chicago Tribune*, June 1, 1924, 5.

216. Evans Clark, "U.S. Indicted as the Most Lawless Country," *New York Times*, November 2, 1924, XX5.

217. Hal Higdon, *Leopold and Loeb: The Crime of the Century* (Urbana: University of Illinois Press, 1999), 167–68.

218. "Lincoln Gardens," *Chicago Defender*, September 1, 1923, 8; "King Oliver's Jazz Band," *Chicago Defender*, August 11, 1923, 7; "King Oliver's Band," *Chicago Defender*, October 6, 1923, 8.

219. Brothers, *Louis Armstrong*, 267; For a musicological analysis of the music of the Hot Fives, see Gene Henry Anderson, *Original Hot Fives Recordings of Louis Armstrong* (Hillsdale, NY: Pendragon Press, 2007).

220. Armstrong, *His Own Words*, 132.

221. Ogren, *Jazz Revolution*, 54.

222. Will Layman, "The Permanence of Pops: Louis Armstrong and American Music," *Popmatters*, February 3, 2013, www.popmatters.com.

223. Brothers, *Louis Armstrong*, 7.

224. Sudhalter, *Lost Chords*, 57.

225. Richard M. Sudhalter and Philip R. Evans, *Bix: Man and Legend* (New Rochelle, NY: Arlington House, 1974), 101.

226. Benny Green, "Bix Beiderbecke," in *Reading Jazz*, 824; Gunther Schuller, *Early Jazz: Its Roots and Musical Development* (New York: Oxford University Press, 1968), 187.

Chapter 7

227. Zorbaugh, *Gold Coast and the Slum*, 91.

228. Franklin Rosemont, *The Rise & Fall of the Dil Pickle Club: Chicago's Wild 20s!* (Chicago: Charles H. Kerr, 2013), 58.

229. Zorbaugh, *Gold Coast and the Slum*, 115.

230. Frank O. Beck, *Hobohemia* (Rindge, NH: Richard R. Smith, 1956), 68–69.

231. Roger A. Salerno, *Sociology Noir: Studies at the University of Chicago in Loneliness, Marginality and Deviance, 1915–1935* (Jefferson, NC: McFarland, 2006), 100.

232. Liesl Olson, *Chicago Renaissance: Literature and Art in the Midwest Metropolis* (New Haven, CT: Yale University Press, 2017), 41.

233. Kenan Heise, "Fanny Butcher Knew the Giants of Literature," *Chicago Tribune*, May 17, 1987.

234. Roger A. Bruns, *The Damndest Radical: The Life and World of Ben Reitman, Chicago's Celebrated Social Reformer, Hobo King, and Whorehouse Physician* (Urbana: University of Illinois Press, 1987), 16.

235. Rosemont, *Rise & Fall*, 20–21.

236. Drury, *Dining in Chicago*, 188–89.

237. Rosemont, *Rise & Fall*, 25.

238. Zorbaugh, *Gold Coast and the Slum*, 100.

239. Zeitz, *Flapper*, 121.

240. Steven C. Tracy, *Hot Music, Ragmentation, and the Bluing of American Literature* (Tuscaloosa: University of Alabama Press, 2015), 101; Rosemont, *Rise & Fall*, 29.

241. Rosemont, *Rise & Fall*, 76.

242. Beck, *Hobohemia*, 81.

243. Rosemont, *Rise & Fall*, 89.

244. For a survey with many illustrations of Chicago art between the World Wars, see Elizabeth Kennedy, ed., *Chicago Modern, 1893–1945: Pursuit of the New* (Chicago: Terra Museum of American Art, 2004). See also Maggie Taft and Robert Cozzolino, eds., *Art in Chicago: A History from the Fire to Now* (Chicago: University of Chicago Press, 2018).

245. Powell, "Becoming Motley," 110.

246. George Hutchinson, ed., *Cambridge Companion to the Harlem Renaissance* (New York: Cambridge University Press, 2007); Richard J. Powell and David A. Bailey, *Rhapsodies in Black: Art of the Harlem Renaissance* (Oakland, CA: University of California Press, 1997).

247. Jontyle Theresa Robinson and Wendy Greenhouse, *The Art of Archibald J. Motley, Jr.* (Chicago: Chicago Historical Society, 1991), 38.

248. Ibid.

249. Ibid., 33.

250. Amy M. Mooney, *Archibald J. Motley Jr.* (San Francisco: Pomegranate, 2004), 18.

251. *Chicago Tonight*, "An Interview with Valerie Browne, Motley's Daughter-in-Law," www.chicagotonight.wttw.com.

252. Quoted in Phoebe Wolfskill, *Archibald Motley Jr. and Racial Reinvention: The Old Negro in New Negro Art* (Urbana: University of Illinois Press, 2017), 2.

253. Christopher Robert Reed, *Knock at the Door of Opportunity: Black Migration to Chicago, 1900–1919* (Carbondale: Southern Illinois University Press, 2014), 228.

254. Wolfskill, *Motley Jr. and Racial Reinvention*, 119.

255. Ibid., 140.

256. Mooney, *Archibald J. Motley Jr.*, v.

257. Amy M. Mooney, "The Portraits of Archibald Motley and the Visualization of Black Modern Subjectivity," in *Archibald Motley*, 21.

258. Olson, *Chicago Renaissance*, 122–36.

259. Darlene Clark Hine and John McCluskey Jr., *The Black Chicago Renaissance* (Urbana: University of Illinois Press, 2012), 177.

260. "Making Good," *Chicago Defender*, February 28, 1925, A10.

261. Mooney, *Archibald J. Motley Jr.*, 50.

262. Olivier Mesplay, "Motley's Paris Missed Opportunities," in *Archibald Motley*, 84.

263. According to historian Tyler Stovall, "twelve Black American artists of note" studied in France during this period. (Tyler Stovall, *Paris Noir: African Americans in the City of Light* [Boston: Houghton Mifflin, 1996], 64.)

264. Powell, "Becoming Motley," 144.

265. Wolfskill, *Motley Jr. and Racial Reinvention*, 33.

266. Robinson and Greenhouse, *Art of Archibald J. Motley*, 17.

267. Mooney, *Archibald J. Motley Jr.*, 63.

268. Hine and McCluskey, *Black Chicago Renaissance*, 177.

269. Powell, "Becoming Motley," 120.

270. William B. Scott and Peter M. Rutkoff, *New York Modern: The Arts and the City* (Baltimore: Johns Hopkins University Press, 1999), 140.

271. Roi Ottley, "Top Negro Artist Works in Factory Job," *Chicago Tribune*, December 2, 1956.

272. Randy Kennedy, "Whitney Museum Acquires Major Work by Archibald Motley," *New York Times*, January 11, 2016.

273. Ogren, *Jazz Revolution*, 103.

274. Clifford Terry, "The Glory Days of Chicago Radio," *Chicago Tribune*, March 4, 1979, F28.

275. Elizabeth McLeod, *The Original* Amos 'n' Andy*: Freeman Gosden, Charles Correll and the 1928–1943 Radio Serial* (Jefferson, NC: McFarland & Co., 2005), 19.

276. Ibid., 26.

277. Ibid., 28.

278. Mel Watkins, "What Was It About *Amos 'n' Andy?*" *New York Times*, July 7, 1991.

279. Nahum Daniel Brascher, "35,000 Cheer *Amos 'n' Andy* at Bud's Picnic," *Chicago Defender*, August 21, 1931.

280. McLeod, *Original* Amos 'n' Andy, 41.

281. Ibid., 108.

282. Kapilow, *Listening for America*, 61.

283. Bart Andrews and Ahrgus Juilliard, *Holy Mackerel!: The* Amos 'n' Andy *Story* (New York: E.P. Dutton, 1986), xvii.

284. Melvin Patrick Ely, *The Adventures of* Amos 'n' Andy*: A Social History of an American Phenomenon* (New York: Free Press, 1991), 7.

285. John Dunning, *On the Air: The Encyclopedia of Old-Time Radio* (New York: Oxford University Press, 1998), 531; WGN's station manager Henry Selinger originally floated the idea of a serial titled *The Sudds* (later renamed *Good Luck Margie*) but couldn't find a sponsor and, after that, turned to Phillips. In that sense, Selinger can be credited with the creation of the soap opera concept. (See Robert C. Allen, *Speaking of Soap Operas*, [Chapel Hill: University of North Carolina Press, 1985], 110–13.)

286. Jim Cox, *The Great Radio Soap Operas* (Jefferson, NC: McFarland, 2008), 253; In 1970, Phillips was quoted as saying, "I'm not part of the feminist movement….I still believe that the home, the family, is the core of society." (Clarence Petersen, "Writer Plans Book, Plots New Serial," *Chicago Tribune*, March 17, 1970, B19.) She went so far as to say, "Women are happier if they can feel dependent and dominated," and her serials almost always had strong male characters. (Carol Kramer, "Irna Phillips, Queen of Soaps, Visits a Noted TV Family," *Chicago Tribune*, March 19, 1969, C15.) Phillips never married but adopted two children. She had previously conceived a child out of wedlock. The father abandoned her, she lost the baby and she was unable to have more children.

287. "High Court Bars Appeal in Suit over W-G-N Play," *Chicago Tribune*, February 14, 1941, 12.

288. Phillips herself reportedly detested the terms *soap opera, washboard weeper* and *detergent drama*, which were all used to describe her genre. (Larry Wolters, "Critic Glances Back at 30 Years of Radio and TV," *Chicago Tribune*, August 23, 1959, N12.)

289. In the 1930s and 1940s, some thirty soap operas were produced on Chicago radio. Some of the others included *Ma Perkins*, *The Romance of Helen Trent* and *Mary Noble, Backstage Wife*, which was memorably spoofed by the comedy team of Bob (Elliott) and Ray (Goulding) as *Mary Backstayge, Noble Wife*. (See Terry, "Glory Days.")

290. Lynn Liccardo, "Vita: Irna Phillips," *Harvard Magazine* 115, no. 3 (January–February 2013): 35.

291. The website of the Harry Stephen Keeler Society offers a wealth of information on Keeler and *10 Story Book* (www.site.xavier.edu). The most helpful was the article "The 10 Story Book Story," by Chris Mikul.

Chapter 8

292. See Michael K. Bohn, *Heroes & Ballyhoo: How the Golden Age of the 1920s Transformed American Sports* (Washington, D.C.: Potomac Books, 2009).

293. Harris, *Chicagoan*, 177.

294. Jeff Davis, *Papa Bear: The Life and Legacy of George Halas* (New York: McGraw-Hill, 2005), 53.

295. Ibid., 55.

296. John M. Carroll, *Red Grange and the Rise of Modern Football* (Urbana: University of Illinois Press, 1999), 108.

297. Ibid., 117–18.

298. "Abe Saperstein Dies; Gained World Fame with Globe Trotters," *Chicago Tribune*, March 16, 1966, C1.

299. "Globe Trotters '5' in National Pro Cage Tournament," *Chicago Tribune*, March 9, 1940, 24.

300. Fay Young, "The Stuff Is Here," *Chicago Defender*, March 23, 1940, 24.

301. This game is considered so momentous that a book has been written about it—John Christgau, *Tricksters in the Madhouse, Lakers vs. Globetrotters, 1948* (Lincoln, NE: Bison Books, 2007).

302. Robert Peterson, *Cages to Jump Shots: Pro Basketball's Early Years* (Lincoln, NE: Bison Books, 2002), 105.

303. Baldwin, "Midnight was Like Day," 76.

304. Paul DeBono, *The Chicago American Giants* (Jefferson, NC: McFarland, 2007), 1.

305. Peter Golenbock, *Wrigleyville: A Magical History Tour of the Chicago Cubs* (New York: St. Martin's Press, 1996), 220.

306. Clifton Blue Parker, *Fouled Away: The Baseball Tragedy of Hack Wilson* (Jefferson, NC: McFarland, 2000), 22.

307. Bill Chastain, *Hack's 191: Hack Wilson and His Incredible 1930 Season* (Guilford, CT: Lyons Press, 2012), 46.

308. Roberts Ehrgott, *Mr. Wrigley's Ball Club: Chicago and the Cubs During the Jazz Age* (Lincoln: University of Nebraska Press, 2013), 207.

309. Chastain, *Hack's 191*, 161.

310. For years, Wilson was credited with 190 RBIs in 1930, but in the 1970s, some baseball statisticians discovered that Hack had not been credited with an RBI he had gotten in the second game of a doubleheader on July 28, 1930. Major League Baseball was slow to convince, but in 1999, Wilson's total was corrected, and the mark was set at 191.

311. Miller, *Supreme City*, 376.

312. Steven A. Riess, "Closing Down the City: The Demise of Boxing and Horse Racing in Chicago," in *Sports in Chicago* (Urbana: University of Illinois Press, 2008), 47.

313. Mel Heimer, *The Long Count* (New York: Atheneum, 1969), 204.

314. Ibid., 88.

315. James P. Dawson, "Tunney Always Master," *New York Times*, September 24, 1926.

316. Don Maxwell, "Rickard Sure Chicago Will Land Bout," *Chicago Tribune*, July 29, 1927, 15.

317. Heimer, *Long Count*, 244.

318. Ibid., 250.

Chapter 9

319. Cheryl R. Ganz, *The 1933 Chicago World's Fair: A Century of Progress* (Urbana: Univ. of Illinois Press, 2008), 34.

320. Tracey Deutsch, "Great Depression," in *Encyclopedia of Chicago* (Chicago: University of Chicago Press, 2004), 360.

321. Lisa Krissoff Boehm, "The Fair and the Fan Dancer: A Century of Progress and Chicago's Image," *Chicago History*, summer 1998, 44.

322. Hope, *Art Deco Architecture*, 202. See also Robert W. Rydell and Laura Burd Schiavo, eds., *Designing Tomorrow: America's World's Fairs of the 1930s* (New Haven, CT: Yale University Press, 2010).

323. Schrenk, *Century of Progress*, 9.

324. Chicago Tribune staff, *A Century of Progress: A Photographic Tour of the 1933–34 Chicago World's Fair* (Chicago: Midway, 2015), 8.

325. Schrenk, *Century of Progress*, 214, 218.

326. Ganz, *1933 Chicago World's Fair*, 71.

327. Hope, *Art Deco Architecture*, 19.

328. For more information on Sally Rand's life and career, see William Elliott Hazelgrove, *Sally Rand: American Sex Symbol* (Guilford, CT: Lyons Press, 2019). By all accounts, Rand was entirely nude behind the feathers, although Hazelgrove cites a contradictory report from a policewoman who said she used greasepaint, a saline covering for the breasts and a padding of silk and maline (a kind of mesh). In the bubble dance, however, she was unquestionably, in Hazelgrove's words, "totally nude."

329. Ganz, *1933 Chicago World's Fair*, 23.

330. "Hammond Asserts Chicago Will Be U.S. Air Center," *Chicago Tribune*, December 26, 1920, F3.

331. "2 Mile Throng Hails Air Race Parade in Loop," *Chicago Tribune*, July 1, 1933, 1.

332. Guillaume de Syon, *Zeppelin!: Germany and the Airship, 1900–1939* (Baltimore: Johns Hopkins University Press, 2002).

333. Michael McCarthy, *The Hidden Hindenburg: The Untold Story of the Tragedy, the Nazi Secrets, and the Quest to Rule the Skies* (Guilford, CT: Lyons Press, 2020), 243.

334. "Balloon Rises a Mile; Falls," *Chicago Tribune*, August 5, 1933, 1.

335. "Picard Predicts Planes Will Fly in Stratosphere," *Chicago Tribune*, March 5, 1933, 5.

336. Schrenk, *Century of Progress*, 15; "Great Fair Will End Tonight," *Chicago Tribune*, October 31, 1934, 1.

337. "Throngs Mingle in Gay Carnival on Final Night," *Chicago Tribune*, November 1, 1934, 1.

INDEX

ABOUT THE AUTHOR

Joseph Gustaitis is a Chicago-based freelance writer and editor. He received his bachelor's degree from Dartmouth College and his master's degree and doctorate in history from Columbia University. He is the author of many popular history magazine articles. After working as an editor at *Collier's Year Book*, he became the humanities editor for *Collier's Encyclopedia*. He has also worked in television and won an Emmy Award for writing for ABC-TV's *FYI* program. His previous books are *Chicago in 50 Objects, Chicago's Greatest Year, 1893: The White City and the Birth of a Modern Metropolis* and *Chicago Transformed: World War I and the Windy City*.

Visit us at
www.historypress.com
....